The Complete Guide to

and

Strategic Planning

for **Voluntary Organisations**

SECOND EDITION

Alan Lawrie

DIRECTORY OF SOCIAL CHANGE

Published by
The Directory of Social Change
24 Stephenson Way
London NW1 2DP
tel: 020 7391 4800, fax: 020 7391 4804
e-mail: publications@dsc.org.uk
from whom further copies and a full publications list are
available.

The Directory of Social Change is a Registered Charity
no. 800517

ISBN 1 900360 87 X

British Library Cataloguing in Publication Data
A catalogue record for this book is available from the British
Library

Designed and typeset by Lenn Darroux
Cover design by Lenn Darroux
Printed and bound by Page Bros, Norwich

Acknowledgements
I am grateful to the many people who I worked with as either
a trainer or consultant who have helped to shape and
challenge my ideas about strategy and planning. I would also
like to thank the Directory of Social Change for supporting
this project and to thank Jan Mellor for help and support
throughout.

CONTENTS

1 Introduction

In the seven years since the first edition of this book, strategic and business planning has become an established part of the managerial and organisational life of voluntary organisations. Funders look to business plans for reassurance that an organisation has thought through its future plans and has the organisational capacity to deliver them. The range of opportunities open to voluntary organisations and the increased demands placed on organisations mean that having a clear strategy and realistic plan can be a critical tool in determining an organisation's future.

This book offers a range of tools and techniques to aid the planning process. New in this edition is material on the planning process, managing risk and on implementing the plan. The book avoids producing a blank plan for people to simply fill in the gaps.

Two important lessons learnt over the past few years are that the process by which the plan is developed and agreed is a central factor in how useful it will be. Also in many ways writing the plan is the easy bit – the hard task is implementing it, keeping to it and managing the change involved.

● What this book is about

This book is about three things.

1 It aims to help voluntary organisations make clear decisions about their future direction and priorities.
2 It introduces some tools for strategic planning and management.
3 It explains how to draw up and use a business plan.

● Why think about business plans?

There are several entry points to the book's subject:

1 The tougher funding climate and the growth of a contract culture have led some funders to require the production of a business plan before they consider a funding application. For example, any application to the Community Fund for a project with a budget in excess of £200,000 (£100,000 for the International grants programme) has to supply a business plan with the completed application form.

Business plans have their roots in the private sector and are an essential requirement in persuading lenders to back an enterprise. In recent years, like many other management concepts, they have crossed from the profit-making sector to the not-for-profit sector.

2 A recognition by many voluntary organisations that the constant rate of change and consequent uncertainty means that the organisation cannot stand still.

Many managers and increasingly some trustees are expressing the need to clarify what their organisation is about, decide what is and is not a priority for the limited resources that exist and set out a direction for the organisation's future. This kind of management is different from dealing with the day-to-day demands of making sure that the organisation keeps operating. Strategic management is hard. It requires clear thinking, clarity of purpose and the capacity to win others' commitment to the process and convince them that it is not some academic or pie-in-the-sky exercise.

3 The arrival at a point where decisions have to be made about the organisation's future.

A director of one charity described her role as like 'riding a rollercoaster that never arrives anywhere but only gets faster'. Changes in legislation, new funding, short-term priorities and new ways of working mean that organisations can easily become reactive to external events and be pulled into activities that either do not fit with the rest of the organisation or are a departure from their original aims. Those charged with the management and direction of the organisation need to take a grip on what they are doing. They need to decide where they are going and not simply respond to external events.

All organisations are going somewhere. The future direction could be about the organisation getting bigger or smaller, working in a particular way or doing more or less of a particular activity. The main theme behind this book is that the people who are charged with managing a voluntary organisation need to ensure that they set the direction and agree strategies for where they want to be.

● Why create a plan?

> *'If you don't know where you are going you are sure to end up somewhere else.'*
> Mark Twain

There are many reasons not to draw up a business plan or think strategically.

- Just to keep operating on a day-to-day basis is often enough of a struggle.
- The language of organisational planning is often offputting.
- The word 'business' might be objectionable to some people.
- Planning in a period of constant change can be difficult.
- There is a fear of finding that the goal posts keep moving.
- The organisation may lack skills or resources to implement the plan.

The following six points explain the thinking behind this book and might suggest reasons why voluntary agencies should spend valuable time on this process. You may find it helpful to work on exercise 1 on p.5 at this point.

A paradox about planning

There is a paradox about planning. The harder it is to plan, the more important clear planning becomes. Uncertainty about funding, lack of clear direction, a reliance on what was done in the past as the basis for deciding what to do next, and a vision that stops at the end of the current financial year mean that an organisation can easily become motionless. It spends its time hoping that things will get better. In effect, it becomes governed by what it did in the past rather than what it wants to do in the future. It becomes predictable and paralysed in a rapidly changing world. At some stage someone needs to be bold enough to suggest a direction to go in and agree a plan for achieving it.

Direction planning rather than a detailed blueprint

In the 1960s and 1970s large corporations and public agencies invested heavily in corporate planning. These planners produced comprehensive ten-year documents that even in more stable times became quickly out of date – or in some cases were out of date the day that they left the printers. Our capacity to predict the future accurately is very limited. This book is concerned with helping organisations *clarify* their long- and short-term goals, *explore* possible future possibilities and *make a case* for why others should have

confidence in their organisation. It is the process that is important rather than the product.

The process and the results matter, not what it is called

The idea of producing a business plan sometimes causes cynicism amongst a staff team. Is it just another imported management fad that someone has picked up on a course? How the process is managed and how people are involved in it has a considerable bearing on the result. Later in this book the difference between first order change and second order change is explored. First order change is when an organisation or individual appears to be doing something differently. Second order change is when we start behaving differently and genuinely commit ourselves to the process of change. Many business plans get stuck at first order change. A plan is produced by a few people, it is published, briefly discussed, filed away and quickly forgotten about. This book is concerned not only with producing a credible plan, but also with ensuring that the plan feels real and relevant to people in the organisation. Whether it is called a business plan, a strategic plan or a forward plan is not important.

The dangers of short-termism

Political changes, annual budgets and short-term funding can make any notion of planning difficult. Part of thinking strategically is to keep in touch with day-to-day realities and opportunities, but at the same time to focus on future needs and directions. The one thing that is certain is that everything will remain uncertain. Secure and committed long-term funding is doubtful and difficult to achieve. Political and economic stability is unlikely with constant reorganisations, friction between central and local government and a chronic shortage of funds. The profile and expectations of an organisation's users are unlikely to become fixed. There is a real danger of voluntary organisations losing a longer-term perspective, becoming driven by short-term demands and only dealing with what is urgent rather than what is important. Just having a short-term perspective could threaten the existence of a voluntary organisation.

During research for this book, a local authority officer with responsibility for grant aiding local voluntary groups said, 'Most of the organisations I deal with would be very easy to cut, and if cut, could close quickly. They are geared up from April to April. They are fearful of taking on longer-term commitments. They employ their staff on short-term contracts (that in practice are often renewed). They have no contingencies. They operate almost as if they expect to be closed down at a moment's notice.'

More and more managing is about accepting uncertainty as a norm, but having the confidence to chart a longer-term direction.

FUNDERS AND BUSINESS PLANS

Funding bodies, statutory purchasers and commissioners and lottery distribution bodies are increasingly asking for business plans as part of the funding process. In research for the second edition of this book many funders were reluctant to go on the record about how they used or analysed business plans. However, contact with a variety of funders identified six main ways in which they use business plans:

1 To understand the idea behind the organisation or bid

The business plan should explain the context, vision and background to the organisation's work. The plan should help to paint the bigger picture and stress the outcomes that the organisation is interested in achieving. The Community Affairs manager of a large commercial company explained that, 'We often ask for a business plan to help us to understand the context and learn more about the organisation's other work.'

2 To ensure that the project has been fully worked out

The plan needs to make funders feel confident that the organisation has exercised sound practice in developing project ideas, costed its work properly and made realistic assumptions about potential income, support, demand and backing.

3 To check that the organisation is being realistic

The plan needs to strike a balance between being ambitious and also being realistic. All commitments and targets in the plan must be backed up with a cogent action plan that shows that

they can be delivered and also that their progress and results can and will be monitored.

4 To ensure that the organisation has thought about possible risk

All plans and endeavours involve some sort of risk. A business plan needs to show that the main potential risks have been identified and evaluated. The plan should show that the organisation has systems, processes and contingencies to prevent and monitor potential risks and enable it to act should they occur.

5 To check that the organisation has the capacity to deliver

A plan must show that the organisation has the management ability to ensure that the plan can be delivered. The plan needs to show that the organisation has the skills, experience and organisational ability to organise and implement the plan. A programme manager for a government initiative commented that, 'plenty of organisations have good, creative and relevant ideas; the business plan needs to convince us that the organisation has the management ability and experience to turn it from an idea into something that delivers'.

6 To understand the longer-term picture

The plan should show that the organisation has taken a longer-term view and is not just going from one event or funding opportunity to another. The plan should show that as well as having short-term strategies and plans, the organisation has thought about the longer-term need and future of its work.

Good planning builds on what you do already

All too often, plans degenerate into a wish list of how we would like things to be, in a perfect world. The frameworks and ideas suggested in this book aim to make sure that any plan takes into account the realities of the organisation in its present situation. You need to ensure that the plan is realistic and sets out clear steps for its implementation. Too often business plans only consist of catchy mission statements without any real evidence that the organisation has worked out how to move forward.

Making the case for the organisation

Often a voluntary agency suffers from a credibility gap. The outside world sees it as being made up of well intentioned amateurs. Funders insist on rigorous and bureaucratic controls on how 'their' money is being spent. Sometimes this rubs off on the staff and volunteers who fail to see fully the effectiveness and efficiency of their efforts or that they are achieving incredible results with minimal resources. A central part of a business plan is to make the case for the organisation. It sets out the track record of the organisation, demonstrates that it has effective systems, people and processes in place and shows that it can deliver results. Voluntary organisations are increasingly being called upon to

show (often through producing a business plan), that they will be a reliable partner in a contract or funding agreement. The process of drawing up a business plan often helps an organisation to value itself more and be more 'assertive' with the outside world.

● The planning process in outline

Stage 1: *clarification of the purpose and mission of the organisation* is about ensuring that there is a clear sense of direction and agreement about the core values that unite an organisation. The decisions reached in this stage should act as an anchor for the rest of the process. Chapter 3 suggests how an organisation can renew its overall purpose, considers the dangers of simply being driven by what was done in the past and gives some practical hints on drawing up a mission statement.

Stage 2: the *information gathering* process is an attempt to take stock of the organisation to date. Chapter 4 looks at ways of collecting information about the organisation's current activities, its financial and management performance, and also suggests ways of predicting how services might develop. It looks at the external environment, and considers how future trends and events might impact on an organisation's future. Chapter 5 reviews the financial information that is needed to plan accurately. It looks at ways of costing work, managing cash flow and at the strategic management of finance.

OUTLINING THE PLANNING PROCESS

The planning process has six key stages

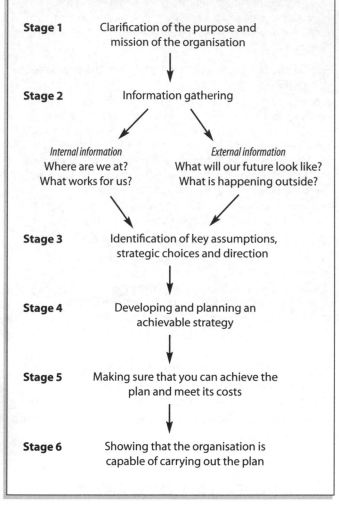

Stage 1   Clarification of the purpose and mission of the organisation

Stage 2   Information gathering

Internal information
Where are we at?
What works for us?

External information
What will our future look like?
What is happening outside?

Stage 3   Identification of key assumptions, strategic choices and direction

Stage 4   Developing and planning an achievable strategy

Stage 5   Making sure that you can achieve the plan and meet its costs

Stage 6   Showing that the organisation is capable of carrying out the plan

Stage 3: considers how to use this information to *identify key assumptions, strategic choices and direction*. This stage, discussed in chapter 6, is a critical one. Informed by a review of internal and external trends, key people in the organisation need to identify choices open to them, evaluate them and agree a direction. This is often a painful process as it usually involves saying what an organisation will stop doing or will not get involved in.

Stage 4: *developing and planning an achievable strategy* is about making realistic choices about the future and creating a coherent plan. Chapter 6 suggests several processes for developing a strategy.

Stage 5: *making sure that you can achieve the plan and meet its costs* is about the feasibility of planning. Chapter 6 also looks at how to work from the priorities agreed in the previous stage, draw up clear objectives for each one and identify the organisational and management processes needed to meet the plan.

Stage 6: *showing that the organisation is capable of carrying out the plan* requires the organisation to show that it has in place the structures, systems and skills needed to implement the plan. Chapter 7 suggests various sources of evidence that an organisation can use in its plan and shows how this information can be used to persuade funders and others to back the organisation.

Chapter 8 gives guidance on writing a plan and provides a template and content list for a plan.

Chapter 9 demonstrates the importance of making sure that the plan is implemented, looks at how it can be used to steer and change the organisation and suggests how managers can use, monitor and update the plan.

Sources of further help – a reading list and software resource guide – are provided at the end of the book.

▼ **Exercise 1**

DIFFERENT REASONS FOR BUSINESS PLANNING

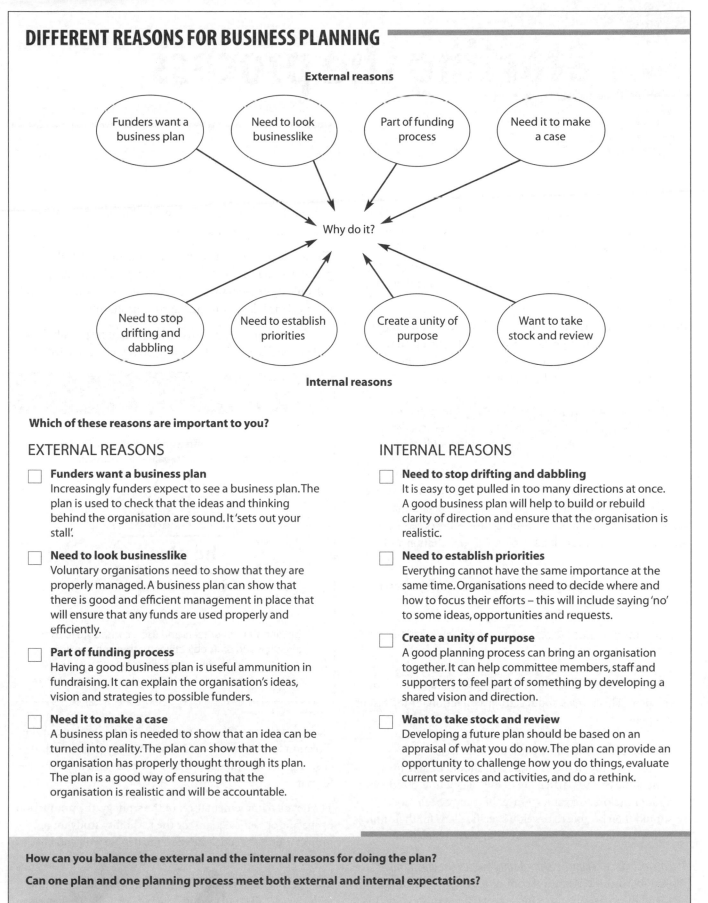

External reasons

Funders want a business plan

Need to look businesslike

Part of funding process

Need it to make a case

Why do it?

Need to stop drifting and dabbling

Need to establish priorities

Create a unity of purpose

Want to take stock and review

Internal reasons

Which of these reasons are important to you?

EXTERNAL REASONS

☐ **Funders want a business plan**
Increasingly funders expect to see a business plan. The plan is used to check that the ideas and thinking behind the organisation are sound. It 'sets out your stall'.

☐ **Need to look businesslike**
Voluntary organisations need to show that they are properly managed. A business plan can show that there is good and efficient management in place that will ensure that any funds are used properly and efficiently.

☐ **Part of funding process**
Having a good business plan is useful ammunition in fundraising. It can explain the organisation's ideas, vision and strategies to possible funders.

☐ **Need it to make a case**
A business plan is needed to show that an idea can be turned into reality. The plan can show that the organisation has properly thought through its plan. The plan is a good way of ensuring that the organisation is realistic and will be accountable.

INTERNAL REASONS

☐ **Need to stop drifting and dabbling**
It is easy to get pulled in too many directions at once. A good business plan will help to build or rebuild clarity of direction and ensure that the organisation is realistic.

☐ **Need to establish priorities**
Everything cannot have the same importance at the same time. Organisations need to decide where and how to focus their efforts – this will include saying 'no' to some ideas, opportunities and requests.

☐ **Create a unity of purpose**
A good planning process can bring an organisation together. It can help committee members, staff and supporters to feel part of something by developing a shared vision and direction.

☐ **Want to take stock and review**
Developing a future plan should be based on an appraisal of what you do now. The plan can provide an opportunity to challenge how you do things, evaluate current services and activities, and do a rethink.

How can you balance the external and the internal reasons for doing the plan?

Can one plan and one planning process meet both external and internal expectations?

2 Starting the process

The process by which the plan is developed and prepared has a critical impact on its successful implementation. Practical experience consistently shows that the sooner that people potentially affected by change are involved in the process, the more likely it is that change will be implemented and followed through.

In planning, there is a tendency for a few select individuals to isolate themselves from others, produce a detailed plan written in an inaccessible management speak and then become frustrated when no-one takes the plan seriously.

> *'The finest plans are often spoilt by the pettiness of those who are supposed to carry them out, since even emperors can do nothing without the support of their soldiers.'*
> Bertolt Brecht

However, it often seems as if the more people that are involved, the harder it is to manage the process. Meetings become longer, difficult decisions are avoided, the process gets delayed, and innovation is strangled by so-called consultation and consensus.

One way to resolve this problem is to think of the process as having three levels.

1 *A downward direction setting out boundaries and criteria for the plan*
   Trustees and managers need to agree the mission and core values. They need to set a broad organisational context for the plan. This level is about setting a direction for the rest of the plan.

2 *Direct input from frontline workers and volunteers*
   People working in the organisation should be able to contribute to and participate in the 'big picture' discussions about mission and values. Once these have been set they should then be able to develop specific plans for their unit or department in the context of the overall direction.

3 *Lateral team working both inside and outside the organisation*
   Groups of staff, users, and committee members can work together to carry out specific aspects of the process such as

identifying future trends or exploring possible future scenarios for the organisation.

The whole process of involvement, consultation and participation needs to be tightly managed. If not, the process will quickly degenerate into endless meetings and many bold ideas will be killed by unmanaged consultation.

Careful timetabling, effective delegation of responsibilities and external help with the process may well be needed.

THE PLANNING PROCESS

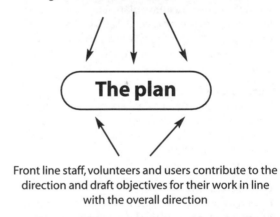

Management committee and senior managers set organisational mission, values and direction

The plan

Front line staff, volunteers and users contribute to the direction and draft objectives for their work in line with the overall direction

Managers need to take the responsibility for setting out the direction for the organisation, agreeing key priorities and ensuring that the plan is produced to time and in a cohesive format.

The detailed implementation of the strategy, the production of specific or tactical plans, or the feasibility study for a project is often best delegated to the people who will have to work on it (and therefore know most about it).

Managers need to ensure that what they produce is in line with the overall strategy of the plan, is realistic, challenging and achievable.

It might also be feasible to involve people who do not directly work in the organisation. Users, carers, supporters and even funders might bring a valuable insight and stop an organisation becoming complacent or inward looking. External consultants can also be engaged to help with the process.

A housing project had two different experiences of producing a business plan. Its first attempt, motivated simply because the Housing Corporation requested it, was the product of hard labour by the director and the finance manager working together. Few people ever referred to the plan or felt that they had any connection to it.

The next attempt was different. A joint team made up of two committee members, the director, the finance manager and one person from each of the project's three teams produced a mission statement and carried out a review of internal and external developments. The next management committee meeting agreed a brief paper from the director setting out likely assumptions and suggesting five core priorities. For the next six weeks the three work teams had to draw up and cost detailed and measurable plans for their team's work. The director's role was to act as a coach for them in this process, sometimes pushing them further, but often making sure that they were being realistic. The final plan was produced by a small team led by the finance manager.

The project's director commented that his role 'had been more about thinking about the big picture than about the detail. I had to "hold the ring" on the process and make sure that the plan was an integral product produced on time. It was very difficult for me to stand back and not take the plan over. Two early benefits have been that people now do refer to how their work fits into the plan; and each team now has a work plan which they monitor but feel a commitment to, as they were the main force in setting it'.

● Seven common business planning mistakes

1 Seeing the plan only as a financial document

Often business plans are delegated to the finance manager or treasurer to write, with the expectation that they will produce a document full of cash flow projections, budgets and balance sheets. Although financial projections are essential elements of a business plan they are only part of it. The plan needs to set out the vision, direction and priorities for the organisation and then go on to explain how such a plan can be funded. The budget and financial projections should follow on from the strategy and not dictate it.

2 Seeing it only as a marketing or fundraising tool

A business plan can play a crucial role in winning and securing funds for an organisation, but it should not be regarded simply as a piece of fundraising publicity or a marketing document. Although it might play a part in convincing a funder to back a project, for a plan to have any credibility or worth it is important that the plan belongs to the organisation and has not been produced for the funder. In showing a plan to a possible funder you are showing them your thinking, your ideas and assumptions that underpin the organisation.

3 Too much detail

Some business plans go into incredible detail. Managers produce plans that spell out in precise detail who will do what, exactly how much will be spent on each item and when things will be done by. Such action planning does have a place, but it is limited. Often it is not possible to produce detailed plans for more than the next six to twelve months. Circumstances change, the level of resources might vary and new issues and demands might emerge. The organisation's purpose and the strategic direction for the next period needs to be clear. The precise detail of implementation needs to be planned for as the organisation develops. Too much detail can obscure the key messages of the plan.

4 No ownership of the plan

The process of developing the plan needs to be one that involves the people who will be affected by it or might have to carry it out. The plan has much more chance of being implemented if staff and other key people feel that they have contributed to it, helped to shape it or at the very least been kept in touch with the process of developing the plan. If they are not involved and the plan is suddenly dropped on them then there is a good chance that they will not feel any particular commitment to change or respond to it.

5 Basing it entirely on what you do now

Often in planning, 'where we are now' feels like a logical place to start. When we draw up a budget we are inclined to use the current budget as the basis for the new one. If all a plan does is to roll forward current services, activities and work then a chance is missed to rethink and evaluate the pattern of services. The plan could be criticised for being driven by past assumptions, past needs and past ideas. The business planning process should provide a structured opportunity to evaluate the organisation's pattern of services and activities against the overall mission and need.

6 Limited horizons

Short-term funding, changing political agendas and regularly changing external demands can work against longer-term planning and strategies. It is easy to fall into short-termism and drift from idea to idea, issue to issue and possibly crisis to crisis. However, organisational survival is not enough. The plan is an opportunity to renew and update the organisation's original founding vision and idea. Such a process can reposition the organisation and help readers to appreciate the organisation's role and distinctive contribution. Do not assume that people who work for the organisation or the people who fund it understand the vision and big idea behind it.

7 Avoiding difficult issues

All organisations have weaknesses, suffer from setbacks and make mistakes. A business plan should not gloss over such issues. If it ignores or does not mention current or past weaknesses it may raise suspicions that the plan lacks an honest and full appraisal of the organisation's development to date. The plan can show a level of maturity and credibility by drawing lessons from the causes of weaknesses and setbacks and by showing that the organisation now has the capacity and skills to either prevent them or overcome them.

● Agreeing objectives for the plan

Often there is cynicism or a lack of confidence about the planning process. Most of us have had enough experience of plans that create paper and lead to no action. One starting point is to agree some objectives for the business planning

process itself. The task of agreeing these objectives might help to clarify the internal and external reasons why a plan is needed and create an opportunity to measure its value over time.

Although it is generally much better to work out your own objectives for business planning, the following list may be helpful:

- To clarify long-term aims.
- To relate all activities to aims.
- To develop a realistic future strategy.
- To make measurable plans.
- To link future developments in the external environment to internal change.
- To convince financial backers that the organisation is credible.

Exercise 2 on p.14 can be used to help you identify your objectives.

A starting point for the process itself is to deal with the often held belief that strategic planning is impossible. The management writer Henry Mintzberg talks about how all organisations are moving in some direction even if they do not know it or have planned it. This is sometimes called an emergent strategy.

SIX KEY MESSAGES THAT A BUSINESS PLAN SHOULD CONVEY

1 That the organisation has given itself a thorough review
The plan should show that there has been a process of rethinking and evaluation. It should show that the original aims are still relevant and that all activities and services have been reviewed and evaluated.

2 That the organisation has considered the impact of external changes and developments
It is important to show that the organisation is in touch with the environment in which it operates. The plan needs to show that the effects of key trends and changes external to the organisation have been considered and that the organisation is ready to respond to them.

3 That the organisation has thought through its strategy
From reading the business plan, the reader should be able to understand the direction chosen by the organisation and the key priorities for the next period.

4 That the full costs, organisational implications and potential risks are clear
The plan needs to show that the people running the organisation have fully costed it and have made sensible assumptions about future patterns of expenditure and income. The plan should refer to potential risks and indicate the kind of management action needed to avoid them or deal with them should they happen.

5 That the organisation has the managerial capacity to deliver the plan
Funders need to feel that the organisation is in safe and reliable hands. The plan needs to show that the organisation has the track record, skills and capacity to use funding properly and ensure delivery of the plan.

6 That there is a plan of action to ensure that the business plan gets implemented
The plan should indicate that there is a very clear management or action plan that sets out the short-term actions and work needed to get started on delivering the plan.

This chart shows the emergent strategies of a youth agency, i.e. how things change over time.

ALL ORGANISATIONS ARE CHANGING ALL THE TIME

Trend	Probable reason	Strategic questions
Less outreach work – now only working with those who come to us.	Pressure of keeping the centre open for ten sessions – funder says that is what is important.	What should be the balance between the centre and field work?
More in-depth work with fewer young people.	Two workers have trained in counselling and want to practise it.	Is this what we are supposed to be doing?
More young black women using centre.	Possibly because we employed a woman worker who is black.	What would happen if she left?
More work with 13–16 age group.	Because older age group are into other things.	Who should be our target groups?
More time on fundraising.	Funders will not pay core costs.	Should we find better ways of making our case?
Doing more work on drug misuse.	Because there are funds available for this work.	How could this develop? Do we want to do more or less of this?

A useful exercise is to ask participants to think back over the past few years and to try to identify what sorts of direction the organisation has moved in and is currently moving in. Discussion should focus on what has driven the organisation, what has controlled it and what choices have been subconsciously made by individuals and teams.

The exercise can help to illustrate the point that although we cannot always control the detail, the organisation is moving and it is better to chart its path then let it happen by accident.

● Leading the planning process

How best to lead the business planning process needs some thought. In many respects the process determines the usefulness of the exercise. The process can help people to learn, identify options and understand the chosen direction.

A badly designed and managed process can produce a plan that no-one feels any commitment to and is likely to gather dust on a shelf.

The following are some ideas for developing a useful process.

Identify who needs to be involved

Start the process by mapping out who should be involved in the different stages of the planning process. Some people may need to be involved throughout. Some might just need to be referred to or involved in specific parts. Consider both internal and external stakeholders. Internal stakeholders might include staff, volunteers, regular users and trustees. External stakeholders might include funders, partners and possibly future users. Be clear about what status is given to people in the process – are you asking them to approve the plan or simply input their views?

Establish a common language

Spend time at the start ensuring that all who are to be involved in it understand the language of business planning. Make sure that people understand the key concepts and the processes involved in putting the plan together.

Help people to see why you are doing it

Often only a few people understand the context that the organisation operates in. It is worthwhile spending time explaining the internal and external reasons for doing the plan. Even if the main reasons for doing the plan are forced on the organisation (for example, funders want a plan), it is useful to stress how the plan is an opportunity to evaluate the organisation and develop future ideas.

Start with a learning process

To develop future strategies we need to have a good grasp of the organisation's current position and the wider world in which it operates. In some organisations staff only see their bit of it and know little of what other parts of the organisation do. Often committee members have a very limited insight into the organisation. They rely upon formal reports or a working knowledge of the issues that might be quite dated. To help people see the whole picture and understand the realities that the organisation faces, a series of briefing or information sharing sessions might be needed.

Do not assume agreement or basic understanding

Often we assume that just because people work or are involved in the organisation, they appreciate or even know about its purpose and aims. Often people have very different views about the organisation's purpose and values. All plans and strategies need a common starting point. It is useful and

THE BUSINESS PLANNING PROCESS

List the people who need to be or should be involved in the business planning process. A useful technique is to draw a diagram of all the groups or individuals that have (or could have) a stake in the process. An advice agency produced the diagram on the right. The next stage is to identify what level of involvement they need to have in the process and then the way in which they should be involved (see below).

Group	Level of involvement	Method of involvement
Regular donors	medium	Contact to see if they would like an input. Invite to comment on draft.
Local authority	medium	See how we could be affected by their neighbourhood renewal strategy. Use councillors on management committee as contact.
Staff team	high	Staff to draft plan. All staff to attend away day.
Volunteers	high	Volunteers invited to away day. Suggest that one volunteer should be on drafting team
Management committee	high – will approve plan	All committee to attend away day. 2/3 committee members to be on drafting team.
Our national network	low	Ask them about national picture and external trends.
Community legal service	medium	Find out about their local strategy and plan.
Other advice centres	medium	Find out about their future plans. Suggest meeting to discuss future strategy and potential cooperation.
Regular clients	medium	Run a focus group to get their views on the agency. See if they are interested in being more involved.
Occasional clients	medium	Produce questionnaire and option sheet on how the agency could be improved.
Solicitors who we refer to	low	Tell them that we are involved in a planning process and ask if they want to be involved.
People who refer clients to us	medium	Ask them for their advice and ideas on how we might develop.

In planning the process three issues are important:

Be clear about decision making

Often when a consultative process is set up issues of power and responsibility can become confused. People need to be aware of the nature of their involvement. Are they being asked to make a decision or are they being consulted? At the start of the process be clear when, how and by who will decisions be made.

Give time – but don't let it drag

All planning processes need time. However, giving too much time to the process can drag the plan down – people get bored by countless meetings, planning days and re-drafts. It is worth designing a process that has a clear timetable setting out the different stages and how much time will be set aside for involvement and consultation.

Avoid the lowest common denominator

Sometimes managers are so keen to avoid a conflict that they adopt a weak or ill-defined position that no-one actively supports and that no-one opposes. Trying to please everyone might make for a quiet life in the short term, but often simply stores up conflicts. The planning process should present conflicting views as different options and choices to be evaluated and resolved by a clear decision.

sometimes revealing to get people to give an instant response to the question 'What is this organisation for?' – often people will give quite different responses. In one agency one person described the purpose as being 'to develop partnerships with the local authority'. In the same discussion a colleague described it as 'to campaign against the local authority'. Confusion about purpose and values can make planning very difficult and will often cause conflict.

Make it a participative process

Give thought as to how to get people creatively engaged in the process. Commitment to a plan often comes from involvement in producing it. A process of active consultation and involvement might include away days, team reviews, getting people to draft elements of the plan and asking people to gather information, identify options and evaluate possibilities.

Be clear about the process

The process needs to be planned. At the start people need to know who will make decisions about the plan and the extent of their involvement in the process. Often conflicts occur or people feel let down if a consultation process is badly managed or implies that the people being consulted have a final say.

Consider external help

Engaging a consultant to help in the process might be useful. A skilled consultant can play three roles. They can facilitate the process by leading discussions, ensuring effective participation and helping to reach agreement on issues. They can provide an external insight by challenging prevailing thinking and ensuring that difficult issues are properly dealt with. A consultant can also act as a coach to the people responsible for putting the plan together. A consultant can provide technical expertise on issues such as costing and also help to ensure that the plan is clear and actionable. A consultant needs to understand the organisation's background, culture and context. It is important that the consultant supports or facilitates the process. The plan must belong to the organisation and not the consultant.

Make sure that the process does not drift

Time needs to be set aside to develop the plan. People need time to go through it and be involved. However, there is a tendency for the process to drift and lose momentum. A useful idea is to agree a time in the organisation's calendar to spend time on the plan. Committees and staff should be asked to ensure that they put time aside to work on or contribute to the plan.

● Strategy and management committees

Management committees clearly have an important role in business plans and agreeing future strategies. As trustees they are responsible for the proper governance and operation of the organisation. However, committee members often have only a token involvement in the planning process – they are confined to simply rubber stamping the plan. A coordinator of a community development agency described how she spent three hard weeks drafting a business plan and then presented it to her management committee. The committee's only input into the plan was to spot a typing mistake and suggest a different typeface for the final draft.

Here are five examples of how organisations have developed a useful role for their committee in the planning process.

As the forum to make decisions and shape the plan

As well as approving the final document a committee can help to shape the plan and resolve issues during the planning process. In one agency the management committee made three key decisions during the planning process:

Approving the mission statement
At the start of the planning process, the committee debated the vision and values of the organisation by looking at the agency's original aims and comments from staff and users on what the agency was for. Once the committee had agreed the mission, work could commence on developing a strategy for how best to implement it in the medium term.

Agreeing the strategy
The committee held a special session to debate ideas, options and choices for the agency's overall strategy. Ideas were presented about the main choices open to the organisation – often in terms of 'we could do more of …' or 'we could move into …' After a debate that involved staff and volunteers, the committee agreed an outline strategy of six key aims. All operational and work plans had to fit with the six strategic aims.

Agreeing priorities
In the course of drawing up the plan, many new ideas were suggested for how the agency might develop and improve. These ideas were clustered together and rough costs were attached to them. The committee then grouped them into an 'ABC' list. 'A' items were top priorities which would have first claim on organisational resources and time. 'B' issues were medium priority items and 'C' issues were issues that the committee did not feel that the organisation would make progress on.

Early involvement in the process

The earlier that the committee is involved the more chance there is of them feeling a sense of ownership of the plan and also a responsibility to work to it. Getting committee members actively involved in the process through away days, review sessions and working on early drafts will often create such a sense of ownership.

Cross-organisational teams

One organisation established three teams to gather information to aid the planning process. One team was given the task of finding out what the agency did well – what were its core competencies; the second team was asked to look at changes in user need; and the third team was asked to gather information on what other similar agencies were doing. The teams were made up of committee members and staff. Each team was given a strict deadline of two months to collect information and present a brief report on what it could mean for the plan. The process increased people's awareness of the issues facing the organisation and opened up communication between the committee and staff.

The committee as a think tank

Good committees have a helicopter vision – the ability to rise above the situation and see the whole picture. Some organisations have encouraged committees to act as a sounding board for new strategies. Often committee members can bring an external perspective to the organisation that is valuable or challenging.

The plan as a route map

Once the plan has been agreed the committee should agree how and when it should monitor it. Some monitoring might be a simple matter of reporting on performance and ensuring that the plan stays on track. Time needs to be set aside to review the strategic direction, priorities and goals. A management committee of an arts company has a special agenda item every quarter to review the plan. The committee chair commented that, 'it is an important item – it gives us the chance to stand back, review progress and check that we are still moving in a direction'.

● The language of business planning

Different writers use words like goals, aims and objectives differently. There is no standard textbook definition. The important thing is to ensure that the terms that are used are defined and understood and that they are used consistently.

This book uses four main terms to describe the planning process.

THE LANGUAGE OF BUSINESS PLANNING

The mission

This is a brief statement of overall purpose and values. It is the reason why the organisation continues to exist. It says little about what, how, or when an organisation will do something. A mission statement should be a long-term statement of intent that follows on from the original vision that inspired the organisation.

Strategic aims

These set out the direction for the organisation. They are a statement of the key priorities for the organisation in the immediate to medium-term future. Everything the organisation does should be related back to a strategic aim.

Critical success factors

These are the things that the organisation has to get right in order to complete its aims and objectives. They usually relate to internal processes, systems and people factors.

The operational objectives

These are detailed, costed and timed plans of what the organisation will do under each strategic aim. They set out a work plan for the organisation.

These are all described in greater detail in later chapters.

● How long to plan for?

The question of how long to plan for is a difficult but obvious question. Most business plans produced these days are usually written for anywhere between one year and five years ahead. Various factors will influence how long to plan for. For example it is reasonable to expect a housing association which may be involved in several capital building or development projects to plan for a longer period of time than a campaigning organisation dealing with changing politics, volatile public opinion and legislative timetables.

One approach is to adopt a plan that rolls forward. An organisation might decide that it can be confident that its mission will still be relevant in three to five years' time. It can probably also identify some strategic aims that will take it nearer to its mission that will also last for two to three years. However, it might decide to produce an annual plan listing specific objectives for the next twelve months that will become its action plan.

Planning the planning process

The newly appointed coordinator of the Seagrove Community Education Centre recognised that a business plan was needed to help with funding bids, but also to renew and update the centre's direction.

After discussion within the staff team and the committee, the coordinator proposed a plan and process for drawing up a plan.

The timetable for developing and producing the plan was as follows:

FEBRUARY
Discussion at the centre's management committee on the need for the plan and agreement of a timetable.

MARCH
Organisational planning day. Twelve people – centre staff, sessional tutors and committee members – worked through a series of exercises to review the centre's overall aims and values, review strengths and weaknesses and brainstorm ideas for how the centre might develop over the next few years.

Results of the planning day were written up and circulated to all.

An outline vision and values statement were drafted by the coordinator and two staff members.

Three information-gathering teams were set up to gain feedback from centre users, to research future demand and needs, and to look at developments in funding for community education.

APRIL
Special management committee meeting with staff and some users invited:

- Presentation from the coordinator on the likely prospects and external environment for the centre.
- Agreement of draft vision and values statement.
- Exercise led by independent consultant to agree future strategic priorities for the centre.

After the committee session the coordinator, treasurer and two committee members worked through costings for the centre's future development, made projections of future income based on best and worst case assumptions and produced a draft plan based on the strategic priorities and their assessment of likely resources. The draft was circulated to the committee, staff and users and the coordinator ran a series of briefing meetings for staff and volunteers.

MAY
Planning day. The coordinator and the treasurer presented the plan and groups worked on five questions:

- What will be different as a result of the plan?
- Are the assumptions in the plan valid?
- What will the centre do more of as a result of the plan?
- What will the centre do less of as a result of the plan?
- What changes will be needed in how we work and organise as a result of the plan?

The points made by the groups were incorporated into a final draft which was then submitted to the management committee.

Three particular issues were important about this process:

- The need to help some people to learn about the centre. Some staff and volunteers only knew about their own work, but not about other aspects of the centre's work. Several management committee members knew little about the context or the environment that the centre operated in. A key feature of the information gathering exercise was about helping people to learn and update their knowledge about the issues facing the centre.
- The importance of developing a process that involves everyone, keeps people informed and makes people feel that they own the strategy.
- The need for the people leading the process to facilitate it in such a way as to encourage involvement, but also to ensure that a momentum is built up and that clear decisions are made.

▼ **Exercise 2**

WHY DO IT?

What are your motives for spending time on producing a plan?

Are your motives mainly internally driven ('we want to decide where we are going') or are they imposed on you by external forces (e.g. a funder demands a business plan)?

What do you want the plan to achieve?

What will be your criteria for judging the success of the plan itself and the planning process?

Exercise 3

THE LANGUAGE OF PLANNING

The terms used in this book need some explanation. You might find it useful to note down what these terms currently mean to you. Do they exist in your organisation and who is responsible for them?

Vision

The reason why the organisation was established and why it continues to exist. What does it want to change or protect? What makes it distinctive from other organisations?

Strategy

The sense of priorities and direction for the organisation over the next period. A series of connected aims that set out an immediate direction for all aspects of the organisation.

Mission

The organisation's current sense of purpose and goal. It should also include a statement of organisational *values* – the beliefs and ethics that should hold it together. The mission should be the driving force behind all the activities.

Objectives

The detailed work plan and action plans that will enable the organisation to implement its strategy. They should be clear and measurable and indicate when and how each objective will be carried out.

3 What are we about?

Almost all voluntary organisations will have a written constitution which says something about their aims, purpose or goals. What is written in the constitution is legally what the organisation is for. This seems a logical starting point for any planning exercise. However, sometimes it is insufficient. Constitutional aims and objectives are often written in a legal or archaic language which may not be comprehensible. Some constitutions are drafted to allow a broad range of possible activities within a legal structure. Some were written so long ago that they do not feel like they have anything to do with the organisation.

Mission statements have become increasingly popular as management tools. Perhaps it all started with probably the best known mission statement, that of the USS Enterprise on television's *Star Trek*: 'To boldly go…'

Many organisations have invested time in producing catchy expressions of their purpose. Often the process generates a degree of cynicism. The statement is often little more than a vague slogan, or it has all the certainty of a New Year's resolution.

Sometimes the term 'mission' is met with scepticism. It is seen as being a trendy idea and a quick fix technique. Management trends and fads never seem to stop. Some management experts now talk of 'mission drift', when an organisation has stopped following its original mission and started dabbling in other activities and sidelines.

There is a strong argument for ensuring that all the people in an organisation have the same sense of purpose and vision. Work spent on defining the mission can have the following benefits:

- It sets out a longer-term perspective.
- It can create unity around a common vision and identity.
- It makes it clear for both insiders and outsiders what the organisation is and is not about.
- It creates an overall sense of purpose from which strategy and action can follow.

Exercise 4 on p.21 can be used to help you write a mission statement for your organisation.

Discussion of mission and vision can cause tension and conflict. Some voluntary organisations have become very good at pretending to be all things to all people.

It is not unusual to find different people in the organisation having very different ideas about what is important and what the organisation's priorities should be. Does a community advice centre exist to inform people of their rights? Or to encourage self help? Or to campaign for social change? Or to counsel people with problems? It may well be possible to do all of these things successfully for a period of time. But when it comes to making decisions about future priorities, future targets or future direction, it is important to have a common view of the organisation's purpose and priorities. If the organisation attempts to do everything, it could well end up fragmented and overstretched.

Three activities are useful for discussing and arriving at a common view:

1 Identifying what drives the organisation.
2 Identifying what is (or should be) unique about the organisation.
3 Describing the organisation's work in terms of outcomes rather than activities.

You may also like to work on exercise 5 on p.22 in this context.

TWO BITS OF JARGON

Mission creep
Often as a result of chasing funding, an organisation finds itself going beyond its core purpose and role. New and different forms of work creep in.

Mission drift
If an organisation does not keep an eye on its core purpose it can easily drift. The organisation takes on too many things. It dabbles in areas of work beyond its original brief. It loses its identity and expertise.

CASE STUDY

A misguided mission

The director of a regional museum did not expect much discussion when he tabled his draft mission statement at the quarterly trustees' meeting. The trustees were mainly academics or amateur historians who had little time for management ideas.

The draft described the mission as:

'To be a lively, open and popular educational experience. To display our collection in a creative and exciting way. To ensure that the museum is open and accessible to local people.'

The chair of the trustees expressed concern that there was no mention of scholarly pursuits or of preserving the museum's collection for common heritage. One trustee said that the mission statement would be more suited to a theme park than to a centre for study and historical research.

The director thought back over previous trustees' meetings. There had been some criticism of his proposal to recruit a marketing officer rather than fill a vacant curator's post. Another disagreement was over spending money on an education pack for schools rather than on extending the collection. The trustees showed no interest in his performance measures which showed a steady rise in visitors; they only seemed concerned with the academic credentials of the staff and the quality of the collection.

At the end of the meeting, the director agreed to redraft the mission statement in the light of the discussion. No doubt he would be able to come up with a compromise set of words that would meet his desire to have a lively and popular museum and the trustees' concern for academic excellence.

Three questions worried him.

Would the compromise wording work in practice or was he just avoiding a fundamental difference which should be resolved in a more substantial way?

Was it possible to 'direct' an organisation where people were being asked to face in different directions?

Could the two approaches be brought together or would the conflict continue to boil away, leading eventually to confrontation?

● What drives the organisation?

Voluntary organisations are driven by other things than simply making money. However, with many voluntary organisations run largely or even entirely by paid staff, the term 'voluntary' may come to feel less and less relevant. The term 'not for profit' is often used instead – although it seems odd to describe an organisation by what it does *not* aim to do rather than what it is for!

AVOIDING A GOAL

Six reasons why for not-for-profit agencies, clear goal definition is often elusive:

1 *The fear of accountability.* Having a clear goal increases the visibility of managers. They become more accountable.

2 Many organisations *continue to have projects when they no longer serve the goal.* Winding an activity up can be very painful, so something which accomplishes little is allowed to continue.

3 *Taking on an activity because money is available.* The availability of funding becomes the driving force, not goals or needs.

4 *A fear that management science may replace romance:* 'Won't hard nosed evaluation undermine humanitarian instincts?'

5 A lot of time in voluntary agencies is spent on *tasks which do not fit into any identifiable goal.* Servicing meetings, encouraging goodwill, liaison with other bodies, public relations and meeting requests for information all make it easy for the organisation to be distracted from its mission.

6 The *financial indicators that a profit-making company has are less meaningful in a voluntary agency.* They say little about progress towards the goal.

Philip D Harvey and James D Snyder
reproduced with the permission of the Harvard Business Review

An organisation is usually driven by lots of different things at the same time. One way of looking at it is to identify three possible driving forces:

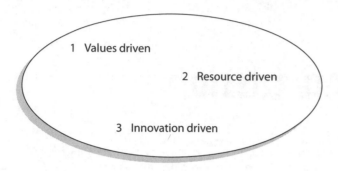

1. Values driven
2. Resource driven
3. Innovation driven

1   Values driven

The *values* driven element is the sense of commitment and shared understanding that holds the organisation together. Values are important in creating a sense of common vision and purpose. However, too much attention to values could lead to the organisation becoming so 'pure' and inward looking that very little ever gets done. Values on their own do not pay people's wages.

2   Resource driven

The *resource* element is the capacity of the organisation to fund and staff its activities. Sometimes this is a drive to get bigger and expand by attracting more and more resources, although there is now a growing recognition that just because an organisation is getting bigger it does not mean that it is any more effective.

3   Innovation driven

The *innovation* element is the organisation's capacity to innovate, take risks and be creative. Many voluntary organisations came into existence to do things that a public sector agency or private company would regard as not sensible practice or too dangerous to invest funds in. Over time, organisations often become safer places and start to reject ideas and innovations that could challenge the status quo. Innovative organisations can be exciting, dynamic and fun. They can also be chaotic, crisis driven and place considerable stress on individuals.

It can be a useful exercise to try to answer the questions that emerge from this analysis:

- What currently drives your organisation?
- Which of these factors do you think is most important?
- How do you manage to combine all the three elements together?
- Which of these are going to be important for the organisation's future?

● What is unique about the organisation?

In a commercial organisation a common marketing technique is to identify a product's USP or unique selling proposition. In simple commercial terms it is what makes one washing powder different from another. The difference can be a tangible one (it performs better) or a matter of perception ('it feels right for me').

It is an interesting exercise to pose the question 'What is unique about our service?' and to try to list the factors that make the organisation distinctive. What would happen if the services were discontinued or the organisation ceased to exist? Would any alternatives be available? Would clients be better or worse off? Would the organisation have to be reinvented?

Possible unique factors include:

- Location and accessibility
- Range of services on offer
- Style of work
- User involvement
- Community involvement
- Locally based
- Independence from other agencies
- Type of client or user
- Use of volunteers
- Cost effectiveness
- Partnerships and collaboration

Some business organisations have formed their mission statement around the characteristics and factors that makes them distinct from other competitors in their market. Work on its 'uniqueness' often helps an organisation to develop a strong sense of identity that holds it together internally and clarifies its purpose externally.

● Outcomes and activities

Many agencies now use a simple model of inputs, activities, outputs and outcomes to evaluate their work, as illustrated in the box opposite.

Most people now recognise that simply undertaking activities and producing outputs without checking on the outcomes is not a productive or sensible use of time and limited resources. Outcomes are hard to identify, often outside of an organisation's direct control and may not be seen for some considerable time. However, outcomes are really what an organisation was set up to achieve and why it should continue to exist.

However well managed, activities and outputs without outcomes are pointless.

INPUTS, ACTIVITIES, OUTPUTS AND OUTCOMES

Inputs	The resources (the money, the time, the people) committed to an activity.
Activities	The services provided. Examples include a training course, an information service or campaign. What the organisation does with the inputs.
Outputs	What and how much gets produced or delivered. Usually expressed through quantitative measures such as '250 hours of training delivered'.
Outcomes	The difference made. What are the short- and long-term benefits of the activity? Does it meet the need? What has changed as a result of the activity?

'There is nothing so useless as doing efficiently that which should not be done at all.'
Peter Drucker

An American book, *Outcome Funding*, by Harold S Williams and Arthur Y Webb, challenges traditional ways of planning, funding and measuring our work. It suggests that our starting point should be the identification of possible outcomes. Measures and milestones towards the outcome can also be identified. Charting these points along the way will allow progress towards the desired outcomes to be monitored. An organisation can then use a range of activities to move towards the outcomes.

Examples of outcomes include:

'Enabling a person to continue to live independently.'

'Establishing a self-help group capable of running its own affairs and sustaining itself.'

'Recruiting and supporting a trained volunteer network.'

Most organisational systems such as job titles, job descriptions and structures are geared around the activity rather than the outcome. Often the energy needed to keep the activity going can start to obscure the outcome. Giving advice, providing a day centre and running a training centre are descriptions of activity and not outcome.

CASE STUDY

Catering or care?

The Millhead charity provided meals on wheels for isolated elderly people living alone. The charity had expanded rapidly over the past few years and had appointed a coordinator to lead a dedicated team of staff and volunteers. The coordinator was soon involved in negotiating contracts with social services and producing the never ending documentation that the social services department demanded.

A year into the post, the coordinator organised a review day with staff, trustees and volunteers. This review session looked at the new quality assurance standards developed at the instigation of social services. They set out various minimum standards about menu choice, food nutrition and catering management. Somehow they did not feel right.

At the end of the session it suddenly occurred to the coordinator that the activity of cooking and delivering food had taken over from the charity's original purpose, to support, care for and befriend isolated elderly people. The means had become the end.

The coordinator explained her feelings to the group. A volunteer talked about what was important to the old people she was delivering meals to, which was knowing that the same person would visit them every Tuesday and Thursday lunchtime and not how often the menu changed or how healthy the meal was. Another talked about how for some old people the actual meal was pretty irrelevant, but what was important was the five minutes of conversation with the volunteer.

After the session, the coordinator worked on a business plan that stressed that what the charity valued was personal care and time with elderly people. These aims could be delivered in several ways such as home visiting, good neighbour schemes or helping relatives to visit more often as well as delivering food.

The mission statement shifted the focus from providing a catering service to a service providing individual care and contact delivered through a variety of activities.

A useful exercise in a planning session is to work through a three-stage process:

1 What outcomes do we wish to achieve?
2 What are the indicators for each outcome and milestones towards its achievement?
3 What are the activities that will help us achieve the outcome?

● Drawing up a mission statement

Informed by work on what drives the organisation, what makes it unique and what outcomes are important, you should now be able to produce a short mission (or vision) statement for your organisation that sets out its purpose.

Good mission statements:

■ are short – no more than forty words;
■ are focused on the value to the user and the relationship with the user;
■ set out the overarching goal of the organisation;
■ describe the values that will influence how that goal will be achieved.

Mission statements do not need to be measurable, specific or targeted. A mission statement by itself is useless. Once agreed it must be followed up by a clear strategy for the organisation and focused objectives for its work.

WHY BOTHER WITH MISSIONS AND VISIONS?

Here are six reasons why it is useful to spend time ensuring that the mission is clear:

A good mission holds an organisation together
The mission statement should help people to understand what the organisation is trying to achieve or change. It should stress the ends rather than the means.

A strong mission should convey the core values
As well as saying what the organisation is for, it should also highlight the core values and ethos that should influence and underpin all that the organisation does. This can help to build a strong and dynamic organisational culture.

It gives a criterion to judge ideas and possible projects against
All activities, services and projects should fit with the mission statement. An important test for a new idea or a new proposal should be that it fits with the organisation's mission.

It gives focus to an organisation
The mission should give a longer-term view. It should help people to see their work in a broader context and help people to understand the point of each person's contribution.

It makes clear the boundary and limits of the organisation
The mission statement should stop the organisation taking on activities that take it beyond its remit and role.

It makes clear what is different about the organisation
The mission should make clear what are the organisation's particular distinctive characteristics. Lots of agencies work with the same client group – in what way are you different?

Exercise 4

WORKING OUT A MISSION STATEMENT

Use this questionnaire to help you work out a mission statement for your organisation.

OBJECTS
What are the objects and purpose of your organisation as set out in the constitution?

ORIGINAL VISION
What was your organisation's original vision, purpose or function?

CHANGING CIRCUMSTANCES
How has that purpose changed? What parts of it are still relevant?

NEW REQUIREMENTS
What needs to be added to bring it up to date?

CENTRAL PURPOSE
What should now be the overriding purpose and direction? What threads hold it together?

RATIONALE FOR CONTINUING
Why does the organisation continue to exist?

CURRENT VALUES
What values hold the organisation together?

IDENTITY AND POSITION
What should be the organisation's identity? How does this relate to other organisations fulfilling similar or complementary functions?

Review your answers. Try to identify key themes.
Now try to draft a mission statement. Keep it to between thirty and forty words.

▼ **Exercise 5**

IS THERE A NEED FOR STRATEGIC THINKING?

The following eight statements were made by a group of managers about to embark on a strategic planning exercise.

Do any of the sentiments expressed sound like your organisation?

1 'We have grown far too fast. Some parts of the organisation are now disconnected from each other.'

2 'We are drifting. The past few years all our energy has been spent on keeping going. We need to establish a new direction.'

3 'We need to establish a common sense of purpose and direction that will hold the project together.'

4 'We could be criticised for trying to be all things to all people. We need to sort out our identity and make priorities.'

5 'The need for our services is growing fast; the resources to meet that need are declining. We are in danger of becoming a crisis, "first aid" service.'

6 'We have been so busy managing that we have missed out on several opportunities to develop new initiatives.'

7 'I have trouble explaining what the organisation is for to outsiders.'

8 'We are in danger of becoming complacent and inward looking. We cannot assume that what we are doing now will be the same in two years' time.'

How would you describe the current state of strategic thinking in your organisation?

Who is responsible for strategy? Where does it happen?

How could it be improved?

4 Gathering information

A business plan must include a realistic assessment of the following:

- Basic management information about the cost of the service and organisational performance.
- A review of likely future trends and scenarios.
- A critical appraisal of the organisation's strengths and weaknesses.

The business plan needs to demonstrate that past history and current performance have been properly evaluated to create the best plan for the future. This chapter looks at how organisations can collect and interpret information and feed it into a plan.

Broadly speaking, the information you need can be divided into three categories:

1 External developments
- The state of the organisation's 'market', i.e. levels of demand for the organisation.
- New ways of working and new developments in the sector.
- New needs and new types of users.
- Developments in similar agencies and statutory provision.
- Known factors that will require a response.
- Predicted factors and trends that could require a response.
- The extent of need.

2 Internal developments
- Recognition of key strengths and weaknesses of the organisation.
- Recognition of key strengths and weaknesses of the services provided.
- The quality of the service.
- Estimates of how the service being provided will develop.
- The needs and expectations of current users.

3 Financial issues
- What your services cost to operate.
- How your costs compare to other agencies.
- Financial income trends.
- Break even and break points.
- Cost effectiveness in relation to outcomes as well as outputs.

● Using a SWOT analysis to get started

A very well-established tool in business planning is a SWOT exercise. It involves participants in identifying and recording:

Strengths
Weaknesses
Opportunities
Threats

In the SWOT exercise, participants record under each heading how they currently see the organisation (its strengths and its weaknesses) and how they see its future (opportunities that could arise and threats that may need to be faced). In using a SWOT exercise the following things often happen:

- People often find it easier to list weaknesses and threats rather than strengths and opportunities. It is often useful to insist that each participant identifies a minimum number of strengths.
- What some people see as a weakness others might see as a strength. One person might describe a day centre as being disorganised and 'not professional' while someone else might see it as being flexible, informal and accessible to clients. Discussion of such different and seemingly contradictory perspectives can be very valuable.
- Often things are neither an opportunity nor a threat. They move around in the middle. A voluntary group might see the change from grant aid to a service contract as something that 'could go either way'. A useful question that leads into strategic planning is 'what do we need to do to make sure that it is a positive opportunity?'.
- People often spend most of their time focusing on what they can do to overcome their weaknesses. However, it is

often worthwhile to spend time on the strengths list and identify the critical factors that lead to something being a strength; and importantly, what does the organisation need to do to keep something a strength and build on it.

A SWOT analysis can be a useful tool for presenting information in a business plan. Exercise 6 on p.33 gives you a template for doing your own SWOT analysis.

● Predicting external trends

> '*The future ain't what it used to be.*'
> Arthur C. Clarke

Our ability to predict accurately how things will be in the next few years is very limited. Traditional planners have tried to sift information and make accurate forecasts of the future. They are usually not very accurate and are occasionally downright wrong! The approach outlined here is more about predicting trends, identifying possible actions needed and agreeing contingencies. Strategic management is about having a clear direction to steer towards and at the same time being able to respond to new developments and changes.

The following five headings are useful to work through to identify future trends.

1 Available resources
What will happen to resources (human, physical and financial) that we currently have? How will our income be affected?

2 Changes in how we work
How might the working methods and styles change? How will practices change? What is new in our field?

3 Changes in demand and needs
What will happen to our current user base? How might our user profile change? Will demand for our service go up or down?

4 Changes in the political/economic arena
What could be the impact of new legislation, changes in policy direction and the state of the economy?

5 Changes in the environment and market
What will happen to other agencies with which we work? Will we cooperate or compete?

After completing the exercise it is useful to note which factors are definite, which are probable and which are possible. It might be useful to see if any themes or links emerge between the different factors.

A further exercise is to look at how the organisation fits with similar organisations doing similar work. This can be useful to predict potential conflicts, and identify possible problems and, perhaps, future alliances.

PREDICTING FUTURE TRENDS AND DEVELOPMENTS

	Available resources	Changes in how we work	Changes in demand and needs	Changes in the political/economic arena	Changes in environment and market
Next 12 months	Fundraising from public will stand still or decline	Some services at breaking point if demand continues		How will community care reforms work in practice and impact on us?	Do we cooperate or compete with similar agencies?
1–3 years	Lease expires on building December 2002 End of three-year funding for development post	External evaluation of project scheduled Active development of user groups	Impact of recession on users and carers	Move to a new local authority structure	Push for a formal quality assurance system
Longer term	Move to contracts rather than grants Unable to predict past three years!	Long-term aim of user control and management	Our clients will get older... Break-up of care arrangements Greater demands for choice and independence	Voluntary agencies having to take over previous statutory services	Potential conflict with other providers over values

CASE STUDY

Looking outside

A locally managed housing advice project carried out this exercise to look at how it related to other agencies which did similar work to it. The following chart is a summary of their analysis:

Agency	Similarities	Differences	Relationship	Strategic issues
Citizens advice bureau	Open door policy. Very busy.	Part of a national service. Deals with more issues than housing. Better public profile. Uses volunteers.	Good cooperation. Some joint training.	Potential for more joint work.
Law centre	Very busy.	Appointments only. Qualified staff. More specialist.	Lost contact due to staff changes.	Need to establish contact. Will they continue to do housing cases?
Housing aid centre at town hall	Only works in housing. Open door.	Directly managed by council. We are independent. They are better resourced.	Poor relationship in the past.	Could we be rivals for funding? Do we overlap? How can we work together?
Solicitors in private practice		They are profit making. Expensive. We are a free service.	Little contact – except when they act for landlords!	As recession hits, might private firms move into this area?

An exercise like this might identify some of the following:

■ Potential for joint working, cooperation, alliances or even mergers.

■ What is unique about the service; this could help in marketing and fundraising efforts.

■ Potential conflicts, most obviously for funds, that may need planning for.

The next stage is to agree a strategy that will respond to the external world and allow some flexibility.

Sources of information about external trends might include:

■ Government statistics (e.g. *Social Trends*, *Household Trends*).

■ Local Authority data on demographic trends.

■ Other people's published plans (e.g. Community Care plans).

■ Research by your own agency and other agencies.

■ Discussions with funders about their plans.

■ Information from clients, obtained formally and informally.

● Predicting internal trends

It is often quite hard to take stock of how the organisation has developed to date, its current performance and significant factors that might affect its future. Often people working in the organisation can be too close to it to see anything objectively. Changes often happen gradually over time and are absorbed without conscious thought.

Good strategic planning needs to include (and make reference to in the business plan) some evaluation of the organisation as it now is.

It is useful to divide this into two categories:

1 Reviewing the organisation's 'programme'
The programme comprises the activities, services and projects of the organisation. Programme evaluation asks: Are we meeting needs? Do the services meet our objectives? How effective are we?

2 Reviewing the organisation's 'process'
Process is the ways of working that an organisation has in place to meet its task. Do the structures, systems and ways of working help or hinder the organisation in meeting its goals? In looking at these issues it is important that the mission of the organisation is clear.

The review has to be in a context of what the organisation stands for. This provides a basis for agreeing criteria by which programmes and processes can be evaluated.

It is also valuable to involve others in this activity. Users, carers, partners and sometimes funders can provide a useful insight and stop the exercise becoming one of self justification.

● Risk management

All organisations encounter some kind of risk. Over the past few years, management thinking has encouraged people to be more methodical about risk; to identify possible risks, to assess the chance of the risk happening and to identify action to prevent or manage the risk. The alternative is to avoid addressing potential risks and try to crisis manage them if and when they happen.

In the business planning process it is useful to review the main risks that could threaten the organisation's ability to deliver the plan. The business plan should show that managers have thought through the risks facing the organisation and have in hand a series of plans to prevent them and manage them.

A simple exercise is to identify the key potential risks facing the organisation. Risks can be clustered together into six main groups:

Tangible or physical risk
The more obvious risks – such as a crisis caused by fire or flood.

Service delivery risks
Risks involved in delivering the service to the user – say, when a duty of care is broken, bad or illegal practice happens or the service is so poor that the organisation could face legal action.

Financial risks
Risk of fraud or of operating costs suddenly increasing.

Organisational risks
Internal factors such as key staff or volunteers leaving.

Political and reputation risks
A threat to the organisation's good name and standing – if, for example, a local branch gets bad publicity for the organisation as a whole.

Market and business risk
A risk in the organisation's environment – which might come from a change in demand or the entry of new forms of competition.

It is important to keep risk in perspective. One manager commented that the risks involved in his organisation were so great that he wondered why anyone stayed around!

A simple risk management framework is useful in discussing risk and identifying long- and short-term action.

Each risk is assessed against:
- the likelihood of it happening;
- the impact of it;
- action needed to prevent it;
- contingency plans to manage it.

CASE STUDY

Managing risk

The management board of a community regeneration agency identified six key risks that they needed to manage:

	The likelihood of it happening	The potential impact of it	Action needed to prevent it	Contingency plans to manage it
Risk 1: All our funding is short-term – risk that some projects could close in 18–24 months' time.	Medium – depends on our ability to secure new funds or extensions to existing funds.	Critical issue.	Start developing exit strategies for each project. Open discussion with funders.	Must always be developing new projects.
Risk 2: We are dependent on a small team of volunteers – risk that some volunteers might leave.	Medium – need to recruit new volunteers.	Important that we stay a volunteer-based agency – we do not want to be reliant on paid staff only.	Increase volunteer recruitment. Develop volunteer retention plan.	Run volunteer recruitment campaign. Develop succession plan.
Risk 3: Cash-flow risk – as some of our funders pay late or in arrears, we might not be able to pay our bills.	High – increasingly being paid late by the local authority.	Threatens our financial security and ability to pay our staff.	Set up monthly cash flow monitoring process. Discuss with council.	Set up loan facility. Renegotiate payment schedule in service agreements.
Risk 4: Poor relationship with local authority – risk that councillors don't like us and could cut our core funding.	Unknown – hard to know what the council think of us.	Partnership working with the council is essential.	Talk to council officers and councillors to establish how they see us. Invite them to visit us – renew relationships.	Find new contacts in the council who will support and champion our work.
Risk 5: Risk that other agencies might move into this area and start winning contracts.	Medium.	Depends if we cooperate or compete.	Identify who might be moving in – is there a possibility of working together?	Develop strategies on how we can work together and not compete. Work out what we do best.
Risk 6: Our building is old, dilapidated and costly to maintain – risk of safety breach or higher maintenance and repair costs.	Medium.	Could be serious – risk of accident or longer-term risk that building gives off an entirely wrong image.	Do Health and Safety inspection of building. Draw up ideas and plans to improve the building. Set up meeting to discuss our concerns with the landlord.	Depends on response from landlord. If negative, consider building move and set up capital fund.

● Reviewing the programme

In the world of marketing, the idea of a product life cycle is often used to plan how long a particular brand will remain profitable. Products often go through a life cycle described as shown in the diagram:

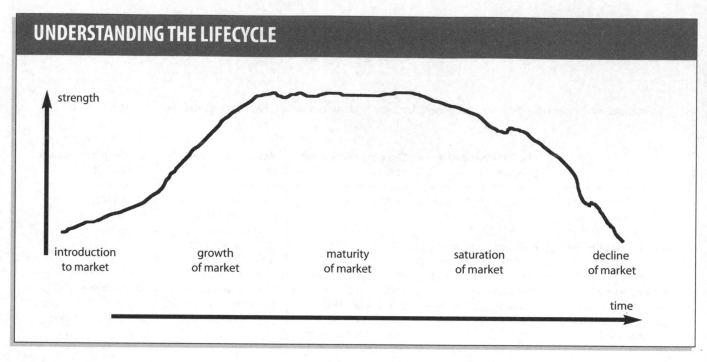

UNDERSTANDING THE LIFECYCLE

Services and products now tend to move through this cycle much more quickly. It is likely that a 'state of the art' computer purchased today will be out of date and need to be replaced by another machine within twelve months. In certain sectors, such as technology and communications, the rate and pace of change is incredible.

Such a rate of change can be very frustrating for managers. As voluntary organisations increasingly operate on a shorter time span and as funding becomes more targeted at the latest 'new' idea, a feeling of change for change's sake can quickly develop. There is a real danger of simply responding to the current flavour of the month and jumping from one idea or project to another. However, it is useful to ask the following questions:

- If we were designing the organisation from scratch, would it have the same services and the same activities as it has today?

- What drives the service? Is it really led by user needs, or is it mainly based on the 'the way that we have always done things'?

- What will each service look like in a few years' time? What resources will it need to operate?

● A portfolio analysis

A useful planning tool is to try to look at an organisation as a collection – or portfolio – of different activities, projects and services. You can then make sure that there is an appropriate balance amongst the activities or projects.

A popular technique used by commercial organisations is the 'growth share matrix' developed by the Boston Consulting Group. With a little adaptation, it can also be used by voluntary agencies.

The matrix is divided into four squares:

Square one: The *stars* of an organisation. These are the activities and services that are particularly strong and have real potential for growth. They are often dynamic, popular and creative. Stars can often fall or turn out to be short lived shooting stars.

Square two: The *question marks* or *problem children*. New activities that take up resources, but, as yet, produce little return. They are often new or innovative projects that might become stars and move into square one or fail and move into square four.

Square three: The *cash cows*. The reliable, safe services and products that have an entrenched position and provide a degree of security. They form a solid base for the organisation.

Square four: The *dogs* or *dead ducks*. These are the activities that take up resources and effort and produce little value in return. Often organisations have problems extricating themselves from such activities.

PORTFOLIO MATRIX

1 STARS	2 QUESTIONS MARKS OR PROBLEM CHILDREN
3 CASH COWS	4 DOGS OR DEAD DUCKS

From working with the model, several strategic choices and options may be identified:

What criteria are being used? A financial perspective might see an activity as being in square three because it can bring in lots of income; whereas someone committed to service development might see it in square four as it is taking up a lot of time just to keep it running.

What should be the balance? What sort of balance do we need between dynamic and risky projects and steady and stable ones? How much effort and time do we put into research and development? What should be the balance between activities that work well now and activities with potential in the future?

How do activities move between boxes? The activities placed in square four (dead ducks/dogs) may at one time have been your stars. How can managers help services move through the matrix and recognise that at some point difficult decisions about their future may be needed?

Exercise 9 on p.36 provides a template for you to do your own portfolio analysis using the Boston matrix.

Strategic questions to ask about the services placed in each box are:

1 Stars
- Why is it a star?
- What are the factors that have placed it in this box?
- How can we replicate these factors elsewhere?
- How long will it be a star for?
- Where will it go next?

2 Question marks or problem children
- How long does this activity need to prove itself?
- How will we know when it is successful?
- How do we manage risk, innovation and possible failure?

3 Cash cows
- Will this activity stay steady and stable?
- Is there a danger of taking it for granted?

4 Dogs and dead ducks
- Do we close it down or renew it?
- What would be the cost of closing this down?
- Why have we let it move into this box?

● Reviewing the process

An important question to ask in any strategic plan is: how does the way that we are organised 'fit' with what it is that we want to do?

Over time, organisations develop procedures, systems and structures for organising their activities. It is easy for job descriptions, departmental structures and internal processes to become restrictive and prevent an organisation changing or thinking strategically.

Often the system can take on a life of its own. A manager employed by a housing agency to develop community based initiatives analysed how her time was being spent. She was alarmed to find that over 50% of her time was spent on dealing with the structure that employed her. Attending and servicing meetings, filling in paperwork, responding to requests for information and 'playing the system' seemed more important than her actual job.

In a planning exercise it is useful to focus on three issues:

1 Is the organisation flexible enough to respond to the changes and uncertainties that we have to deal with?
2 Does the way we are organised fit with our task and our values?
3 Do all aspects of the organisation work together?

CASE STUDY

Youth Development Agency – portfolio analysis

1 STARS Counselling helpline Disability youth group	2 QUESTIONS MARKS OR PROBLEM CHILDREN Health project Computer project
3 CASH COWS Centre based clubs Arts project Sports activities	4 DOGS OR DEAD DUCKS Residential centre International exchange

Square 3 took up most of the organisation's resources. They were the main activities that operated on a week-to-week basis. Over the past five years they had changed little, and as far as the organisation was concerned would continue to serve a useful purpose. One of the activities, the arts project, was causing concern. It was starting to drift. It was attracting fewer young people. Its funder had described it as 'becoming rather predictable'.

Square 4 had two activities that were part of the agency's history. The residential centre, a cottage, was donated to the agency ten years ago. At that time it was, for a short period, a star. For the past two years, it had needed considerable repairs, a new roof and regular visits from the agency's administrator. As a result, it drained resources and because of the poor state of repair few groups ever visited. The international exchange programme had become an annual commitment that the agency undertook 'because it had done it last year'. Few people participated, it often went over budget and took up considerable staff time. However, those who did participate thought that it was very valuable.

The portfolio analysis highlighted six strategic choices for the agency.

1 Innovation was seen as an important role for the agency. How much time and money could it risk in square 2? How much time should it give new ideas to establish themselves?
2 What future is there for the two items in square 1? Could they peak? What if funders lost interest (moved on to other stars), but expectation from users continued to rise?
3 Are we really confident that the items in square 3 are steady and safe?
4 What do we need to do with the arts project? How do we stop it drifting into square 4?
5 What future do we envisage for the residential centre? Do we invest in it, market it and give it a new direction or do we look to dispose of it?
6 Should we continue with the international exchanges? If we move out of this area will we get opposition from those of our members who benefit from it? Could we float it off to someone more skilled in this area?

Square 1 consisted of two new projects that were 'breaking new ground' locally, were picking up considerable media interest and were getting a very good response from young people who the project had traditionally very little relationship with. One of the projects, the counselling helpline, was also attracting interest from a neighbouring local authority who expressed an interest in developing a similar service.

Square 2 had two new projects. A health project that was still very much at a pilot stage. No-one knew if it would work, but it was considered worth investing in. The computer project had been around the organisation for two years. It had attracted little interest from users (or funders) and really was little more than a pipe dream of a particular worker.

The management consultancy firm, McKinsey & Company, developed a useful framework for taking stock of how an entity organises itself. They argued that for an organisation to work effectively, it had to achieve a 'synergy' between seven elements, all of which helpfully began with the letter S.

THE 7-S FRAMEWORK*

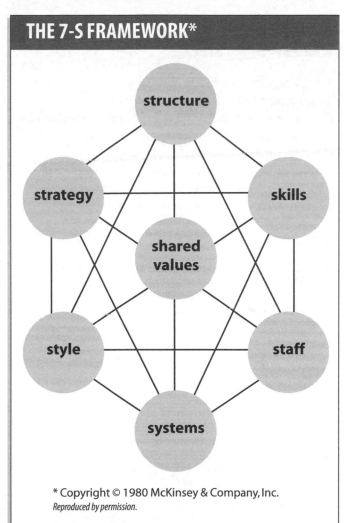

* Copyright © 1980 McKinsey & Company, Inc.
Reproduced by permission.

You can use the 7-S framework to identify weaknesses and shortcomings in how your organisation works by considering the following questions.

Strategy
- Does the organisation have a clear purpose?
- Is the organisation future orientated?
- Do people in the organisation understand its strategy?

Structure
- Does the way that work is divided up make sense?
- Is the structure flexible enough?
- Does it allow good communication between people?

Staff
- Are the right sort of people in the right sort of jobs?
- What sort of employer are we?

Skills
- Do we have the right skills mix to develop in the way we want to?
- Are there any current skills gaps in the organisation?
- How do we invest in the staff that we currently have?

Systems
- Do we have sufficient management control over our resources?
- Do we know what things cost?
- How do we make decisions?

Style
- What is our relationship to our users like?
- Do we present the kind of image that we want to?

Shared values
- Are the organisation's shared values clear?
- Is there a clear agreement about what is important?
- Is there a clear agreement about how we work?

● Using the exercises

This chapter contains a number of exercises that can be used in the business planning process in three different ways:

You can use them on your own to clarify your own thinking and develop your ideas.

You can use them in groups to share perspectives, develop a shared view and help people to exchange views and ideas in a constructive way.

The results of the exercise can be presented in the plan itself.

If you are using the material with a group, some preparation is needed. You need to be clear about the objective and purpose of each exercise and how the issues discussed can be carried forward into the planning process.

The following five points might be helpful to whoever is leading or facilitating any group planning session:

1 People need to feel safe
Participants in a group discussion need to understand why they are doing it. They also need to feel confident that the discussion will be properly led, that people will be listened to and that confidentiality will be respected. The group leader needs to ensure that the group has clear rules to operate to and should watch out for conflicts becoming personal.

2 Feelings are important
Many of the exercises are about making subjective judgements. Often people have a 'gut feeling' why something is a strength or a weakness. Hard facts are important, but there should be space in the process for people to express opinions and then work to a more objective position.

3   *Often there is not a single correct answer*

Understanding different perspectives is important. A treasurer might regard a project as a great success because it is fully funded, covers all of its costs and even brings in some money. Whereas a field worker might regard the same project as dull, lacking in direction and failing to deliver. The important issue is not getting to a single answer, but enabling both sides to see and understand the different perspectives. Once that has been achieved, the organisation is more likely to be able to agree a shared strategy and plan.

4   *Ensure that the discussion moves on*

The group leader needs to help the group move through a discussion. A useful process is to get everyone to work on the exercise individually or in pairs, then to share each analysis, identify points of consensus, discuss differing points, and then move on to identify options for future plans and development. The effective use of questions can guide the group from discussion to analysis to planning:

Discussion points

What do we have in common?
What different perspectives are there?

Analysis

What conclusions can we draw?
Why has this happened in this way?
What learning points can we draw for future actions?

Planning

What options are there for the future?
What kind of strategy is needed?
What would be the first steps in moving this forward?

5   *Make sure the exercise is followed up*

The group leader has a key responsibility to ensure that the discussion is concluded and is followed up. The leader might choose to record the discussion by noting points of agreement and also points of disagreement. The leader should ensure that a process is agreed for feeding the points from the discussion into the business planning process – for example by presenting options for change.

▼ **Exercise 6**

DOING A SWOT ANALYSIS

Set out the strengths and weaknesses of the organisation as you see them.
Note possible opportunities and threats which may emerge in the future.

Strengths	Weaknesses

Opportunities	Threats

▼ **Exercise 6**

▼ Exercise 7

LOOKING OUTSIDE

List all the organisations who do similar work to you. Include organisations in the voluntary, public and private sectors as appropriate. Note what is similar and what is different. What are their particular strengths? Consider the following issues:

What will the future relationship between your and their organisations be? Cooperative or competitive?

Are there any opportunities for joint work and alliances?

Are there dangers of rivalry or other threats?

Organisation	Similarities	Differences	Relationship	Strategic issues

▼ Exercise 8

PREDICTING FUTURE TRENDS AND DEVELOPMENTS

	Available resources	Changes in how we work	Changes in demand and needs	Changes in the political/economic arena	Changes in environment and market
Next 12 months					
1–3 years					
Longer term					

▼ Exercise 9

PORTFOLIO ANALYSIS

Amongst the work of your organisation you will be able to identify projects with different characteristics which contribute in different ways to the organisation's personality and future development. These can be classified in four broad categories:

1 **Stars:** strong projects with real potential for growth, dynamic, popular and creative.
2 **Question marks or problem children:** new or innovative projects, but not yet proven.

3 **Cash cows:** reliable, safe services that provide the organisation with a degree of security.
4 **Dogs and dead ducks:** take up management and financial resources and provide little value for the effort involved.

Now place your organisation's services and projects on the Boston portfolio matrix by allocating each one to one of the four squares.

1 Stars	2 Question marks or problem children
3 Cash cows	4 Dogs and dead ducks

Now answer the following questions:

Is the balance of the portfolio right?	**How do we manage activities in the top two squares?**
How will each of the projects develop over the next year or so? (consider likely demand, trends and income).	**How do we manage activities in the bottom two squares?**

5 Sorting out the numbers

Some business plans consist of little more than financial projections. There has been a tendency, particularly from banks and some larger funding bodies, to ask that the business plan projects income for the next three years, gives a detailed cash flow analysis and shows that the organisation is (and will remain in years to come) a safe and viable concern.

This is often a pointless exercise. Few organisations in any sector can accurately predict their financial position much beyond the next financial year.

However, a business plan needs to show the following:

■ That the organisation is *financially viable* and that it has thought through its financial policy and likely income and expenditure in an intelligent and realistic way.
■ That it has made *sensible assumptions* about its likely financial future.

■ That it has *realistically costed* its activities and taken into account the need for *contingencies*.
■ That it has sufficient *financial controls* to properly manage and plan.
■ That it has coherent *financial management* policies.

Increasingly investors are more interested in the assumptions behind a plan. This involves checking that the financial plan has been properly considered rather than checking every item of anticipated income and expenditure line by line.

This chapter looks at six issues:

1 What financial information do you need?
2 How can you project income?
3 Establishing the break even point and the break point.
4 Establishing what an activity costs.
5 Forecasting cash flow.
6 A checklist of ten financial questions to consider.

SHOWING HOW IT WORKS – WHAT THE BUSINESS MODEL IS

All organisations are based on some kind of model or framework that shows how money can be raised or earned and then used to fund the organisation's work. Often the model is implicit or never described in any detail. In a business plan it is important that readers understand how the organisation intends to fund itself and the assumptions behind the overall financial framework.

In most voluntary organisations income is raised from donations, fees and payments for work done (contracts). This income is then used to fund the work. Increasingly organisations are developing more complex and creative models.

Here is one example. A second one is given overleaf.

1 A counselling centre developed what it described as a cocktail of different forms of income to fund its work. The majority of its income was from a service agreement with a local authority. The centre had been able to develop other income streams such as charging some private clients, delivering an occupational health programme for a large employer and running a series of training courses in basic counselling skills. The centre's business plan set out the different funding and income streams, explained the relationship between them and how income from one area was intended to subsidise another.

Explaining the business model can do three things:

It sets out the assumptions behind the plan
The business model shows the thinking behind how the organisation operates. It shows how the organisation fits together.

It shows the interdependence between different elements
The model sets out how different activities and different income streams relate to each other.

It highlights potential risk
It can show potential danger or exposure to risk. For example, the withdrawal of one relatively small funding source could have serious impact throughout the system.

2 A community arts centre developed a funding model based on three strands:

- Grants and service agreements from public authorities to pay the full cost of the centre's core programme of arts development work with young people. All funding would include an element to pay for the centre's running costs and core staff team.

- The centre would develop a programme of 'Arts in your life' services and products that it could market to schools, local agencies and companies. The programme would be costed to include a contribution to the centre's management costs and any profit made would be used to fund experimental projects or work with unfunded groups.

- The centre would also offer for rent a set of rooms and run a cybercafé and small-scale print shop. These activities would generate income to use to develop new projects.

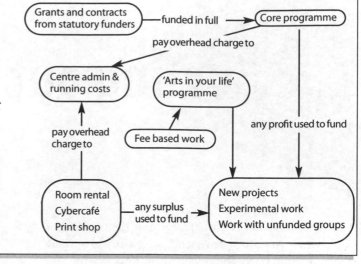

⬤ What financial information do you need?

Many voluntary organisations have delegated financial management entirely to the treasurer or finance officer. It has been their job to manage the 'bottom line', to look after the budget, to keep the organisation solvent and to ensure that reports are produced annually to meet constitutional and legal requirements. Greater emphasis on proper governance and management, changing funding patterns and increased requirements from funders all mean that more attention is being paid to financial management and all trustees and managers are being expected to participate in financial

decision-making. The increased emphasis on financial management is important for three good reasons:

1 The tougher funding climate means that many organisations are facing difficult financial choices.

2 Contracts and service agreements require an organisation to accurately cost and price individual projects and services. In the past, statutory bodies made a grant aid contribution to support an organisation. Contracting is about purchasing a specific service from an organisation at a predetermined price. If the price is wrong the service still has to be delivered.

USING FINANCIAL INFORMATION

This chart describes the main sources of financial information:

	What is it?	What should it tell you?	How can you use it?
The budget	An estimate of income and expenditure for a set period, usually a year.	Where the money should go and where it should come from.	Regular (usually monthly or at least quarterly) reports will show actual income and spending compared to the budget.
The balance sheet	A snapshot of the financial health of the organisation on a particular day, usually the year end.	The current value of the organisation, i.e. the difference between liabilities (money owed) and its assets (what it owns – fixed and current).	The acid test of viability – is the organisation a going concern?
The receipts and payments account	What cash was received and what cash was paid out in a period.	How the organisation is spending and receiving money.	To reconcile spending with the bank account and to monitor cash flow.
The income and expenditure account	The receipts and payments account adjusted to include money owed to it and owed by it – to give a true picture of the organisation's income and spending.	Whether income will meet expenditure.	To indicate the current financial performance.
Statement of financial activities (SOFA)	A summary of all incoming resources and how they are used.	For most charities the SOFA replaces the income and expenditure account – it shows the movement of funds and income and expenditure.	To show how the organisation uses its funds, and the breakdown between direct charitable expenditure, fundraising and publicity costs and management and admin costs.
Cash flow forecast	Timed forecast of when income will be received compared with planned spending.	Whether there are any points when there will not be enough cash to meet outgoing.	To ensure scheduling of income and expenditure.

3 Greater public scrutiny of voluntary organisations is expected. Voluntary organisations need to be open and transparent about how they use their funds and resources.

In putting together the business plan you need to give careful consideration to how much financial information to include. How you present financial information will depend upon two factors:

1 How open you wish to be about your organisation's financial affairs. For example, some organisations negotiating contracts have felt in a weaker position because their potential purchasers have had full details of their financial arrangements.

2 Your ability to be accurate about future financial projections. The further you plan from the present, the less certain your financial projections will be. One organisation produced draft income and expenditure forecasts on the following basis.
- Year one: Monthly projections.
- Year two: Quarterly estimates.
- Year three: A rough estimate of income and expenditure for the year.

Exercise 10 on p.52 provides a 'Financial health check' for your organisation.

How can you project income?

Many organisations are plagued by the short-term outlook of some funders. It is easy to get caught up in an April to April scramble for cash. An essential activity in a business plan is to try to predict income trends in future years.

Possible income sources might include:
- Grant aid from statutory bodies
- Service agreements and contracts
- Grants from trusts and companies
- Public fundraising
- Sponsorship
- Legacies
- Subscriptions and donations from members
- Profit from trading operations
- Earned income from the sale of services
- Hire of resources
- Investment income
- Management fees
- Consultancy fees
- Income from users (such as rent).

PREDICTING TRENDS IN CURRENT INCOME

A community arts agency produced the following prediction of its likely sources of income for the next three years.

Income	Current position	Prediction of trends	Action needed
Council grant from leisure committee	30% of income. Annually agreed. Use not specified.	Will evolve into service agreement. Funding probably stay at same level or inflation plus.	Push for three-year agreement. Sort out a negotiating strategy.
Regional Arts Board (RAB) funding	25% of income. Annually agreed for running costs.	Review by RAB to be carried out this year.	Follow up review. Monitor the changing funding criteria.
Commercial sponsorship for artist in residence	14% of income. Will end this year.	We will lose a management fee of £2,000.	Identify actual loss to central costs. Alternative funding?
Fee earned for local estate work	12% of income. From 4 contracts.	Difficult to predict. Do they cost more than we think? Pricing policy.	Need marketing outside of current network. Review.
Hire of building for events	9% of income.	Bookings falling from previous year's level.	Need to review this area. Need to market it.
Office rented to outside group	6% of income.	Not a realistic rent level.	Schedule rent review.
Donations Miscellaneous income	4% of income.	Will probably stay at this level with minimal effort.	Do we need a fundraising strategy?

This activity quickly identified some issues for the management to address:
- Does it really know what each activity costs?
- Did it properly cost out the full cost of a project or activity before taking it on?

One interesting aspect of this exercise was that no individual in the agency had responsibility for managing specific income. Hire of the building, office rent, donations and sponsorship were all organised on a very ad hoc basis. No one thought about them in a strategic way, but they accounted for 31% of the agency's income.

The process of analysing these income sources is often called a 'sensitivity analysis' in the jargon of business planning. This should consist of three elements:

1 Reviewing current position. How stable has the income been in the past?

2 How do we predict each source of income developing? What is likely to happen to it? What is it dependent on? How reliable will it be?

3 What action is needed to achieve the target? What can we do to secure this income? How can we protect or extend it through better marketing or better negotiating?

Exercise 11 on p.53 can be used as a framework for your predictions

● Establishing the break even point and break point

In a profit-making venture the break even point and the break point are of critical concern. The break even point is the point at which income from trading starts to overtake the fixed and variable costs of the operation.

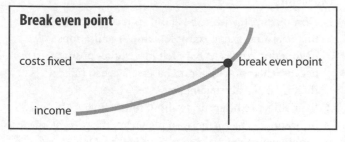

Break even point

CASE STUDY

The community café's break even and break points

A community café calculated that it would have to meet a fixed cost of £85 each week regardless of how many meals they sold. The fixed costs would include rent, wages and payments on hire purchase. As the chart below shows, even if the café sells no meals it still has to pay out £85 in fixed costs. The variable cost is 40p for every meal it makes. This is the additional cost of every meal it sells at 75p.

At 244 meals the café reaches the break even point. Income from sales has overtaken the combined fixed and variable cost. At 244 meals the café moves into profit, the fixed cost remains the same and only the extra variable cost of each meal sold is added to the total cost.

However, there is a point when the growth of the operation means that the ability to respond to growth is inadequate. At

around 400 to 450 meals the café starts to hit break point. The café needs to invest in more equipment, more space and more staff to cope with increased customer demand. If it fails to do this, it is likely that the service will start to suffer. The quality of both the food and the service will be reduced, staff could become stressed and customers might stop coming. The café could be harmed by its own success.

At – or even better, well before – the break point, the café needs to have the cash to expand its capacity to do business. This will add to its fixed costs (taking them to £170 per week) and in the example shown takes the café (hopefully only temporarily) back into a loss. It could have planned for this by setting aside a certain sum each week to cover such expansion and increased cost.

FIXED COSTS: £85 per week	VARIABLE COST: £0.40 (i.e. cost per meal)			PRICE: £0.75	
meals sold	fixed cost	unit cost	total cost	income	profit/loss
450	£170	£180	£350	£337.50	(£12.50)
400	£85	£160	£245	£300	£55
300	£85	£120	£205	£225	£20
250	£85	£100	£185	£187.50	£2.50
244	£85	£97.60	£182.60	£183.40	£0.80
200	£85	£80	£165	£150	(£15)
100	£85	£40	£125	£75	(£50)
0	85	0	£85	0	(£85)

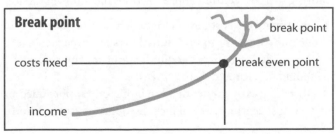

CASE STUDY

Managing the break point

The Morton Family Centre was faced with a dilemma. Over the three years it had been open, cases and referrals were rising by about 15% per year. Word of mouth recommendations, successful publicity work and high quality services had contributed to this increased demand.

At the end of the third year, an external evaluation pointed to four issues that needed attention:

1 The centre did no organised follow-up work with its clients.
2 Workers were increasingly dealing only with urgent cases, rather than working in a preventative way.
3 Time for staff supervision and development was often lacking. High caseloads often meant that workers were too busy to look after themselves.
4 The centre was starting to work only with families referred through social services. This was often seen as quicker and 'more managed', whereas open access work often took up more time.

It was clear that the centre was close to its break point. Client work was becoming less responsive to individual needs, staff were feeling under increasing pressure, waiting time for services had grown to the point where opportunity for early intervention was lost, and internal management systems were starting to crack.

The centre's main strategic issue was how to cope with the increase in demand with no prospect of the necessary increase in resources to cope with it. Two issues were worked on by the staff and management committee:

How to be more effective at saying 'no' to new casework. There was a need to manage the intake routes into the centre, and in particular to explain the organisation's limitations to agencies who referred clients. To some extent, the internal culture of the centre had to change; people often took on impossible caseloads because they felt guilty about saying 'no'.

The second issue was to include in the centre's business plan and in all future funding agreements a series of 'management ratios' that would make sure that the centre did not go beyond its break point. The ratios included:

• Number of clients per caseworker
• Amount of direct time and time for follow up and supervision.
• Number of direct workers and available management time.
• Amount of time for referred work and time available for new work.

A monthly monitoring meeting would act as an early warning system to see if the break point had been reached on any issue.

Break even analysis has always had relevance when a service receives income for every time it gets used. For example, a hostel needs to fill a certain number of beds each night to remain viable. For some, identifying the break even and break point might not be so straightforward.

The break point is that point at which the service reaches capacity. New clients can only be dealt with if extra resources (human and physical) are provided. Every organisation has a point where it becomes viable and certainly a point at which,

if it continues to take on more work, it will have gone past its capacity. Beyond the break point it will then start simply responding and crisis managing. It is worth noting that sometimes the most relevant break points are not to do with cash income. They could include staffing levels, casework systems and physical space.

Discussion of break even and break points for voluntary organisations highlights several important strategic issues:

Many voluntary organisations have a culture that encourages people to go beyond the break point, never say 'no' and somehow manage to provide a service to more people with either the same or declining resources. The long term consequence of this is that a service becomes led only by demand, it only reacts to pressure and sooner or later the quality of work suffers.

The problem of the break point is a problem of success. Demand for the service has outstripped the capacity to supply it. Several studies of small business failures point to growing too fast or growing beyond its capacity as reasons for failure. In many instances managing rapid growth and increasing demand is as hard as managing crisis and decline.

In a profit-making enterprise it should be possible to see the break point approaching, produce a business plan that shows the venture's success, and gain the financial backing to obtain extra financial resources to take it over the break point. When a voluntary organisation reaches a break point it is highly unusual for a funding body to offer additional cash because the organisation is very busy. Several agreements between voluntary and statutory agencies are very clear about the minimum service requirements, but are silent about the point at which the service being purchased reaches break point and a further contract would have to be negotiated. Increasingly, strategic management is about identifying the current capacity of the organisation and managing demand in a fair and equitable way.

What to do when you hit break point

The break point is the point at which demand for the service overtakes the level of resources available to deliver it. Examples might include:

- The number of clients using a service.
- The number of cases, projects and activities that a worker can properly manage.
- The ability of the organisation's infrastructure to manage and support services and projects.

At the break point the following strategies are possible:

- Stop taking on new work – only take on work that you have the resources to do properly.
- Seek more funds and resources – secure new funds that will allow for expansion and will increase the organisation's capacity to deliver.
- Ration the service – reduce the service – limit what users can expect.
- Review existing work – examine existing work – could some of it be brought to a conclusion or gradually reduced?
- Make priorities – decide what is important – withdraw resources from some areas to allocate to others.

An alternative strategy, not recommended but often used, is to ignore the break point and to struggle on. Watch how the organisation changes – the service becomes entirely reactive, developmental work or opportunities are missed and staff become exhausted and stressed.

● Establishing what an activity costs

Traditionally, budgeting in voluntary organisations has been about making sure that there will be sufficient income to meet projected expenditure. The focus has been on getting the 'bottom line' to balance. Changes in funding arrangements, the increased use of specific projects within organisations and an increased unwillingness to pay for core or admin costs has led several agencies to move away from a traditional budget to one which more accurately shows the full cost of a specific activity.

A TRADITIONAL BUDGET FORMAT

Income		Expenditure	
Council grant	____	Salaries	____
Trust & company donations	____	Administration	____
Fundraising	____	Building	____
Sales income	____	Projects expenditure	____
TOTAL	____	TOTAL	____

The budget does not indicate what each activity or service costs. An alternative method of budgeting is called cost centring or activity based budgeting. Several organisations are moving from a traditional budget to a one in which all expenditure is charged to a particular activity or project.

Central to cost centring is the division between direct and indirect costs.

Direct costs are the costs that are only incurred as a direct result of running the particular activity. A project's decision to run education courses would therefore involve the cost of trainers, room hire, course material and probably most of the education officer's time. If it did not run education courses it should not incur these costs.

Indirect costs are the shared organisational costs. They are costs that are difficult to apportion to a specific project or activity. Examples in the case study would be some of the manager's time, some administration costs and some building charges. Increasingly, organisations are finding it hard to obtain separate funding for indirect costs.

Moving to a cost centred budget involves the following steps:

1 Identifying the cost centres to use. This could be related to income sources or to work functions such as particular project, activities or geographic areas. The centres used should be clear and distinct areas.

2 Allocating expenditure that can be directly apportioned to each cost centre. This will include supplies, resources and

people's time. This process could be done on the basis of past usage (for example, 'on average, the rural project uses the minibus for a third of its available time').

3 Agreeing how the remaining expenditure (the things that cannot easily be allocated to a specific cost centre) should be dealt with. In the case study, a fixed formula was used to divide the indirect costs between centres. The indirect cost is a charge to the activity or project to cover the central management or infrastructure costs.

CHANGING HOW WE THINK ABOUT FINANCE

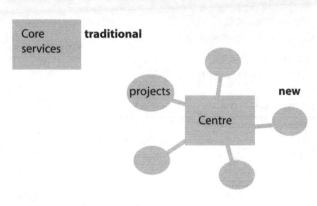

Traditionally, all that mattered was that the organisation's budget balanced – that income covered expenditure. The budget was drawn up using very broad categories – salaries, administration, etc.

Many organisations have moved, or are moving, away from this and are having to develop new forms of structuring their accounts that show the full cost of each activity and project. This change is driven by several factors:

- The movement to funding or contracting for specific projects (rather than giving unrestricted core funding) means that it is necessary to know the full cost of each project.
- The need to ensure that the projects and activities contribute to the organisation's core costs.
- The need for much more accurate management information about what each activity or project fully costs.

Developing a cost centred approach raises several issues.

■ Many voluntary organisations have been very poor at properly costing their work. The cost of spending or using other people's money can be high. Often the costs involved in operating and providing good management have not been properly identified, have been under-costed or even ignored. This can easily lead to a long-term crisis of struggling to do 'quality work on the cheap'.

■ Several organisations which have moved into cost centres have realised that the real cost of an activity is often far more than the grant or contract income that they receive

from a statutory authority. This can raise a policy issue of whether a voluntary organisation should subsidise work carried out for statutory bodies. It may also help negotiators adopt a more assertive approach in future contract discussions. There may be occasions when an organisation takes a strategic decision to take on an activity at below its full cost and either cross-subsidise or fundraise to fill the gap. In the past, the lack of any real costing information has meant that organisations have often drifted into activities without any sense of the financial implications.

■ A negative side effect of the cost centred approach is that it can create an unhelpful competitive tension within the organisation. People in one centre can start complaining that they 'are more profitable' than others. This needs careful management. Cost centres provide management information that can help with making priorities and attaching value to activities. The value of an activity will probably be measured in more than financial terms.

■ In some organisations the issue of what is a reasonable amount to spend on indirect costs as opposed to direct ones has become a controversial one. A hostel manager complained that she had to add on £62,000 to her annual costs to pay for her parent organisation. She doubted if she received anywhere near £62,000 worth of management and central services back in return. In other sectors, reducing indirect central costs has been pursued zealously, either through 'creative accounting' strategies, or through 'downsizing' in which central services and jobs have been cut. Perhaps a more useful approach is to look at how central services can 'add value' to the core projects and activities of the organisation through giving direction, providing support and the delivery of efficient services.

● Explaining the core

There is much concern about the issue of core costs. Many funders are concerned to ensure that resources are used on services rather than diverted into administration and bureaucracy. Some funders impose a strict limit as to how much they will pay for management costs and overall administration, or will only pay for additional or new management costs caused by a new service or project.

The business plan has an important role in explaining and defending the amount spent on core costs. Here are four examples of how to treat core costs in a business plan:

1 Ensure that you are clear about what is a core management cost and what is a service or project cost

Often items that are really concerned with the delivery of services are hidden away as core costs. A review of the core costs of a youth agency showed that several costs that were treated as central core costs should really have been allocated out to projects as direct costs. The agency manager's salary

CASE STUDY

Moving to a cost centred budget – The Community Health Project

The project is a voluntary-run health education project with eight main activities:

EDUCATION & TRAINING
Courses for teachers, health workers on health matters.

'GOOD HEALTH' WEEK
An annual health promotion week.

A RURAL PROJECT
Community health work with isolated communities.

RESOURCE CENTRE
A centre producing and disseminating teaching and resource materials.

HIV/AIDS PROJECT
An awareness campaign on HIV/AIDS issues.

YOUTH PROJECT
Specific health work with 16–22-year-olds.

PUBLIC ENQUIRIES WORK
Enquiry point for a wide range of public calls.

STUDENT SUPERVISION
Placements for students.

The project's staffing is:

	full salary cost
Manager	£30,000
Education officer	£27,000
Information officer	£24,000
Field officer	£24,000
Resources officer	£22,000
Clerk (part time)	£12,000
TOTAL	£139,000

Its current budget is:

INCOME	
Health Authority contract for public information work	£128,000
Trust grant for rural work	£20,000
Government grant for HIV/AIDS work	£14,000
Income from courses	£18,000
Income from sale/hire of resources	£3,000
Student placement supervision fees	£4,000
Local council grant for 'Good Health' week	£10,000
TOTAL	£197,000

EXPENDITURE	
Salaries	£139,000
Administration	£16,000
Resource materials	£4,000
Minibus	£3,000
'Good Health' week	£7,000
Telephones	£8,000
Building costs	£20,000
TOTAL	£197,000

The budget had existed in this format for a number years. However, four reasons prompted the project's treasurer to recommend moving to a cost centred budget:

- The budget did not show the cost of individual activities.
- Funders and purchasers wanted to become more 'project' based.
- There was an urgent need to properly cost and price contracts.
- The project was experiencing difficulty in raising money for core running costs.

AGREEING COST CENTRES

The manager and treasurer reviewed the project's work and identified six cost centres. In future, all of the project's expenditure would be allocated to one of the six centres:

- Education (includes students)
- Resource centre (includes public enquiries)
- 'Good Health' week
- Young people
- HIV/AIDS
- Rural work

The first task was to review the expenditure items other than salaries from the original budget and allocate them to each cost centre. The project's building costs were allocated on a fixed percentage basis (based on a rough estimate of how much space each activity took up). The £7,000 in the original budget for the 'Good Health' week obviously could be allocated as a direct cost to the 'Good Health' week cost centre. A quick review of past purchases from the materials budget indicated how it could be allocated between the six centres. The minibus costs were also shared out on the basis of approximate past usage. Some items, such as the admin and telephone budgets proved difficult to allocate as they were mainly shared items. However, it was agreed that a quarter of the phone bill (£2,000) and an eighth of the admin budget (£2,000) could be allocated as a direct cost to the resource centre's public information work.

Budget Cost centre	Admin £16,000	Materials £4,000	Minibus £3,000	'Good Health' week £7,000	Telephones £8,000	Building costs £20,000	Total allocation
Education		£1,000				£4,000	£5,000
'Good Health' week		£200	£200	£7,000		£2,000	£9,400
HIV/AIDS		£500				£3,000	£3,500
Resource centre	£2,000	£2,000			£2,000	£5,000	£11,000
Youth project		£100	£500			£3,000	£3,600
Rural work		£200	£2,000			£3,000	£5,200
Not allocated, i.e. indirect costs	£14,000	£0	£300	£0	£6,000	£0	£20,300

The next stage was for each staff member to review their work and allocate it in broad percentage terms to the six cost centres. The manager and team secretary recognised that a proportion of their work could not be directly allocated to one of the six centres as it was time spent on project-wide administration, management and development. This time would be part of the indirect costs of the project. The percentage allocation (and cash equivalent) are shown overleaf:

Cost centre	Manager	Education officer	Information officer	Field officer	Resource officer	Clerk	Total allocation
Education	20% i.e. £6,000	70% i.e. £18,900	10% i.e. £2,400			10% i.e. £1,200	£28,500
'Good Health' week	10% i.e. £3,000	10% i.e. £2,700		10% i.e. £2,400	20% i.e. £4,400		£12,500
HIV/AIDS	10% i.e. £3,000		20% i.e. £4,800	20% i.e. £4,800	10% i.e. £2,200		£14,800
Resource centre	10% i.e. £3,000	10% i.e. £2,700	60% i.e. £14,400		60% i.e. £13,200	20% i.e. £2,400	£35,700
Youth project	5% i.e. £1,500		10% i.e. £2,400	20% i.e. £4,800	10% i.e. £2,200		£10,900
Rural work	5% i.e. £1,500	10% i.e. £2,700		50% i.e. £12,000			£16,200
Not allocated Indirect cost	40% i.e. £12,000					70% i.e. £8,400	£20,400
Total	£30,000	£27,000	£24,000	£24,000	£22,000	£12,000	

At this stage only the direct costs have been allocated.

Cost centre	Direct non staff costs	Direct staff costs	
Education	£5,000	£28,500	£33,500
'Good Health' week	£9,400	£12,500	£21,900
HIV/AIDS	£3,500	£14,800	£18,300
Resource centre	£11,000	£35,700	£46,700
Young people	£3,600	£10,900	£14,500
Rural work	£5,200	£16,200	£21,400
Total	£37,700	£118,600	£156,300 (Total direct costs)

Still to be allocated (indirect costs):

      Non staff costs £20,300   Staff costs £20,400   **£40,700** Total indirect costs

      Total expenditure £197,000

The remaining £40,700 – made up of the £20,400 from the salaries budget and £20,300 from the non salaries budget – still needed to be allocated. The £40,700 represents the project's indirect costs. It was shared out between the six centres on percentage formula:

Cost centre	% share	Indirect costs	Direct costs	Total cost centre
Education	20%	£8,140	£33,500	£41,640
'Good Health' week	10%	£4,070	£21,900	£25,970
HIV/AIDS	15%	£6,105	£18,300	£24,405
Resource centre	25%	£10,175	£46,700	£56,875
Young people	15%	£6,105	£14,500	£20,605
Rural work	15%	£6,105	£21,400	£27,505
		£40,700	**£156,300**	**£197,000**

had been treated as a 100% core item, yet the manager spent at least two to three days a week working with young people and delivering services. Are issues such as volunteer expenses, training, publicity and costs of evaluation a core cost or should they be more properly regarded as a direct delivery cost?

2 Show how the organisation can illustrate economies of scale

Often an organisation that manages a range of projects and services can achieve an economy of scale by having a single administrative or management base providing support to a variety of projects. A community development agency illustrated that it provided good value for money by showing that if a project was to become independent, incurring the cost of having to set up its own administration, personnel processes, financial systems and organisational management structure, then the total cost would be significantly more than the management fee charged.

3 Demonstrate that the core functions are well managed

It is important to show that the core functions are efficient, well organised and regularly reviewed. The plan should show that the organisation's systems are relevant to the needs of the service and are tightly managed.

4 Show how the management core 'adds value' to the services and projects

The term 'core' is not a particularly positive or appealing one. The plan needs to show how the organisation's central administration and management add value to rather than take value away from the organisation's work. Examples of added value from the core include:

- providing responsive management and supervision;
- the operation of effective quality assurance standards;
- individual projects being able to access other services and being part of a bigger team.

● Forecasting cash flow

Business planners are often inclined to be very enthusiastic about cash flow forecasts, as many organisations have learnt a hard lesson that an anticipated cash surplus can easily be blown away by budgeted income not arriving on time. Cash flow forecasting is about ensuring that there will always be sufficient cash available to meet anticipated expenditure.

In reality it is very difficult to accurately predict exact income and expenditure patterns and cash inflows and outflows for more than eighteen months ahead. However, a business plan needs to show the following:

- That the impact of cash flow has been considered.
- That cash flow will be managed.
- That the organisation will have sufficient cash reserves to meet its needs.
- That the organisation understands its patterns of cash flow

including seasonal ups and downs.

In looking at a cash flow forecast it is useful to consider the following questions:

- Are there any points at which we will not have sufficient cash to meet our outgoings?
- What is our minimum monthly operating cost?
- How much working capital do we need to pay for expansion and development?
- What could we quickly do to improve our cash flow position in an emergency?

A business plan may indicate the steps taken to manage and improve cash flow.

Tactics might include:

- Writing payment schedules (possibly with penalty clauses) into contracts.
- Monitoring payment of fees and grants.
- Tighter control of people who owe you money.
- Faster invoicing.
- Spreading out expenditure in instalments.
- Delaying some expenditure.
- Delaying payment of certain bills.
- Better banking arrangements.

● A checklist of ten strategic financial questions to consider

The following ten strategic financial questions are useful in appraising an organisation's financial arrangements and financial strategy as part of the business planning process.

1 Do we have sufficient working capital?

Working capital is calculated by subtracting current liabilities from current assets. On a balance sheet, this is usually called net current assets. Every organisation needs sufficient working capital to ensure that cash flow can be managed, to develop new projects, and to cope with unexpected events. Voluntary organisations often live a hand to mouth existence where the slightest financial problem can cause difficulties. Many organisations have not been able to follow up opportunities due to a lack of working capital.

2 Do we know what it costs to operate?

Increasingly, organisations are having to develop accurate costing systems that identify the true cost of a specific activity or service. Costing needs to be accurate and realistic. It should fully take into account both direct and indirect costs and provide regular information that will ensure proper cost control.

3 How do we price our work?

The cost of an activity should be based on rational facts. The price that a service is offered at is usually based on a tactical or

DRAWING UP A CASH FLOW PROJECTION – part 1

A community arts organisation worked out its likely cash flow projection as follows:

	12 months	April	May	June	July	August	September	October	November	December	January	February	March
opening cash balance		£500	£21,130	£14,920	£14,740	£7,640	£1,190	-£980	£14,300	£11,180	£5,160	£3,690	£1,420
INCOME													
Council grant	£30,000	£15,000						£15,000					
Arts Board	£25,000	£10,000						£10,000			£5,000		
Sponsorship	£14,000			£6,000					£4,000			£4,000	
Fee income	£12,000	£2,000					£5,000			£1,000			£4,000
Building hire	£9,000	£900	£700	£500	£300	£100	£300	£500	£1,000	£1,700	£1,400	£800	£800
Rent income	£6,000	£500	£500	£500	£500	£500	£500	£500	£500	£500	£500	£500	£500
Donations/ misc.	£4,000	£400	£350	£350	£250	£250	£300	£400	£350	£350	£300	£350	£350
TOTAL INCOME (monthly income)	£100,000	£28,800	£1,550	£7,350	£1,050	£850	£6,100	£26,400	£5,850	£3,550	£7,200	£5,650	£5,650

48

DRAWING UP A CASH FLOW PROJECTION – part 2

EXPENDITURE													
Salaries	£42,500	£3,220	£3,260	£3,330	£3,500	£3,500	£3,670	£3,670	£3,670	£3,670	£3,670	£3,670	£3,670
Building cost	£13,000	£1,100	£1,000	£1,200	£1,000	£1,000	£1,000	£1,000	£1,600	£1,100	£1,000	£1,000	£1,000
Admin	£18,750	£2,000	£1,600	£1,500	£1,500	£1,400	£1,500	£1,500	£1,600	£1,600	£1,550	£2,000	£1,000
Phones	£3,000	£750			£750			£750			£750		
Festival	£7,000			£600	£200	£500	£1,200	£3,000	£700	£800	£100	£100	
Projects	£7,750	£700	£1,300	£500	£800	£300	£500	£500	£500	£800	£1,000	£350	£500
Equipment	£8,000	£400	£600	£400	£400	£600	£400	£700	£900	£1,600	£600	£800	£600
TOTAL EXPENDITURE	£100,000												
monthly expenditure		£8,170	£7,760	£7,530	£8,150	£7,300	£8,270	£11,120	£8,970	£9,570	£8,670	£7,920	£6,770
closing cash balance (opening balance+ monthly income- monthly expenditure)		£21,130	£14,920	£14,740	£7,640	£1,190	-£980	£14,300	£11,180	£5,160	£3,690	£1,420	£300

marketing decision. Three possible strategies for pricing work are available:

Plus cost

The cost is 'marked up' by a fixed percentage to create some surplus and possibly also to allow some room for negotiation with purchasers.

Under cost

The fee agreed is below the actual cost. The organisation takes on a piece of work in the full knowledge that it will need to subsidise it. Possible reasons include: to attract future work; because the organisation's cash flow demands cash at any cost; or because the organisation is so committed to the activity that it is prepared to invest its own money in it. There may be occasions when an organisation does take on work under cost, but it needs to have very clear reasons for doing so.

The price is set by the market

There is a 'going rate' or an agreed rate for the activity set by the purchaser or by other organisations. The organisation needs to see if it can recover its costs (or even create a surplus) within the price that has already been set.

4   Can we control the patterns of cash flow?

Managing cash flow is important. Ensuring that future funding arrangements take cash flow into account, scheduling income and expenditure, and agreeing payment schedules, can all help to overcome potential cash flow problems.

5   How much does it cost to use other people's money?

The resistance of some funders to contribute to indirect costs or overheads has meant that the true cost of operating has sometimes been ignored. Some organisations have taken on projects where the income only meets the direct costs. The cost of having the project in the organisation is ignored.

6   Is the balance between direct and indirect costs right?

Getting the right balance between project costs and organisational costs can be hard. Some organisations suffer from having an overstaffed and over-resourced centre and an under-resourced front line. What is a reasonable balance between the centre and the projects? Is the centre too large for the current level of project activity? Does it add value to the project work?

7   Are we managing our income as well as our expenditure?

Most organisations have controls over their expenditure that stop them going over budget. Is income also managed? Is sufficient attention paid to ensuring that income keeps to target, that shortfalls are picked up early, and that the future sources of income are carefully researched and managed?

8   What sort of contingency fund do we need?

A contingency fund is an essential part of good financial arrangement. Contingency funds cover unexpected cash flow problems and unforeseen events and circumstances. There has sometimes been a resistance to building one up.

9   How will we replace capital items that depreciate over time?

Most capital items lose value over time. Each year the vehicles or equipment that the organisation owns reduce in value. On a balance sheet this is known as depreciation. The rate of depreciation depends on how long the item is expected to last; a proportion is written off every year and some funds should be allocated to a fund to replace the asset at the end of its useful life. It is advisable to check that there is sufficient money in the replacement fund to meet likely replacement costs and that the depreciation timetable is accurate. One computer training centre found out that their accountant had assumed that their computers would be replaced every ten years, when it was likely that they would last for three years at the very most. Money needs also to be set aside for repairs, refurbishment and decoration.

10   Do we have sufficient financial skills?

Do the in-house financial people (treasurer, finance officer) have full control and are they able to provide regular and accurate monitoring information? Are the external financial advisers (e.g. accountant or auditor) useful in financial planning and aware of tax, VAT and investment issues?

● Ten costs often ignored

The following ten costs are ones which are often underestimated or simply ignored.

1   Start up costs

One-off costs involved with launching or establishing a project. Staff recruitment costs, moving in costs and launch publicity costs are often underestimated or create an early cash flow problem.

2   Slow start costs

Sometimes services start more slowly than anticipated. Organisations that sell their services or receive unit contracts (i.e. when services are paid for on a use basis) can experience below-target performance at what is often an expensive time due to extra costs involved in the service's start up.

3   Marketing costs

Publicity costs, communication and image-building costs are often ignored, leading to poor or amateurish public relations that can cause credibility problems.

4   Working capital

Working capital is money which is not allocated or dedicated. It allows you to develop new projects and to experiment. A lack of working capital means that new ideas and opportunities have to be ignored.

5 Research and development costs

Costs involved in user consultation, needs identification and service evaluation are often expensive and should be built into service budgets and plans, to demonstrate good management practice.

6 Cash flow costs

Many organisations operate to very tight cash flow plans. A delayed payment from a funder or unanticipated expense can easily knock a budget off course. Anticipating cash flow problems and making necessary arrangements to survive a cash shortage can lead to extra costs.

7 Management and administrative costs

An extra project will usually demand extra management and administrative time and space from the main organisation. There is a danger of simply adding projects and activities on until the systems break down. Extra admin time, payroll costs, computer usage and management time all need to be calculated. Volunteer management is another related cost.

8 Replacement and repair costs

Capital items will usually need to be replaced at some stage. Items such as computers, office equipment and other resources will periodically need replacing. Many organisations have a replacement fund which accumulates cash for such costs. Is the contribution to the replacement fund sufficient?

9 Contingency costs

Staff maternity leave, sickness cover, legal costs and emergency repairs are all examples of contingency costs. Some organisations now hold a central contingency fund to which all projects contribute. Some contingency costs can be met by insurance cover.

10 Close down costs

There will often be costs involved in closing down a fixed-term project that need to be built in. These could include evaluation costs, accounting charges, repairs and replacement costs of equipment and buildings and staff costs.

CASE STUDY

A tale of two cultures

In the space of two weeks, the director of a community project had two different discussions about her agency's financial policy.

The voluntary sector liaison officer at the local authority told her that 'concern was being expressed' within the authority that the project's recently published annual report had shown an 'operating surplus' of £7,000. The project had decided to build up a reserve fund equivalent to six weeks' operating costs to cover cash flow, develop new ideas and cover any contingency. The local authority took a dim view of this. Council money was supposed to be spent on local needs, not sit in a bank account. The possibility of 'clawing back' unspent money was mentioned.

A week later a manager from a potential corporate sponsor visited to assess a proposal the project had made. The manager concluded the review by drawing attention to the lack of any forward financial strategy and that a 'well managed organisation should be building up a significant reserve fund for longer-term investment'.

This case raises three issues:

1 The need to educate some funders and purchasers about the necessity for sensible financial management practice. The business plan can play a useful role in this by setting out that a sensible contingency fund is required and explaining how any reserves are earmarked for a specific purpose.
2 The importance of managing the relationship with funders. In the private sector, companies spend heavily on 'investor relations' – a form of internal marketing to stakeholders. Could a marketing strategy help to avoid the frustrations experienced by the community project?
3 The need for a business plan to explain the reasons for policy decisions in a positive and not defensive way.

▼ Exercise 10

A FINANCIAL HEALTH CHECK

This exercise aims to help the planning process by focusing on three issues:

1 The recent and current financial management and performance of the organisation.
2 The importance of developing a coherent financial policy for the organisation.
3 The need to think about finance in a strategic way and not simply a bureaucratic way.

Think about the past few years and future possibilities and answer the following questions:

Financial history

1 How effective has the organisation been at costing projects? Have budgets usually been accurate or have certain costs been ignored or badly estimated?
2 What has been the pattern of cash flow in the organisation? Have there been any regular peaks and troughs?
3 How have costs been allocated in the organisation? Have the indirect costs (i.e. management charges, administrative overheads) been properly recognised and reasonably shared out?
4 What has the balance sheet looked like? What has been the liquidity ratio – i.e. how much cash (current assets) has been available to pay off current liabilities?

Financial management and systems

1 Have there usually been adequate systems of financial control within the organisation?
2 Do budget holders receive information which is up to date, relevant and accurately monitors planned income and expenditure to actual performance?
3 Does the organisation's financial system give accurate information on what specific services and projects cost (including their contribution to the organisation's indirect costs)?
4 Are any particular costs volatile or highly variable? How will this affect the business plan? Can they be controlled better?
5 Are there sufficient financial skills within the organisation to:
   - control income and expenditure?
   - accurately cost projects?
   - develop and project financial plans?

6 Do you anticipate any modifications to your budgeting or accounting systems? What improvements are needed?

Financial policy

1 Is sufficient income set aside for reserves and contingency?
2 What proportion of the organisation's turnover would be a reasonable amount to carry as a reserve or contingency fund?
3 Is sufficient income set aside to cover depreciation and for replacement costs?
4 Are the full costs of operating services and projects known?
5 Is the balance between central charges and direct project costs a fair one?

Financial projections

1 Over the next two years can you predict how income sources will develop?
   - Which income sources do you predict will decline?
   - Which income sources do you predict will increase?

2 What are your minimum operating costs in a month?
3 How flexible is your income?
4 What proportion of your income is:

   - 'earmarked' or committed for a particular expenditure (i.e. its use is restricted)?
   - dedicated from one year to another (for, example, salaries for permanent staff, contractual obligations to suppliers)?

5 Is there sufficient flexibility available to the organisation about how it uses its income?
6 Does current spending accurately reflect current priorities?
7 What costs could be reduced?

   • Direct project costs
   • Indirect organisational overheads

Financial strategies

1 Can you anticipate any significant changes in your organisational cost base over the next few years?
2 How effective is your charging or pricing policy?
3 Is there a coherent policy behind the charges that you make for your services to statutory purchasers, funders and consumers?
   - What sort of pricing strategy do you currently use?
   - How does this compare to other organisations doing similar work?
   - How might this change?

Identifying a financial strategy

After reviewing your answers to the above questions, try to answer the following points:

- What financial choices does the organisation have?
- If the organisation was starting again what would be different about how it organises its finances?
- What are the financial priorities for the organisation?

▼ Exercise 11

PREDICTING TRENDS IN CURRENT INCOME

In column A, list all your current sources of income. In column B, note the proportion of your income this particular source currently represents. Also note any other relevant details; for example, if the income is scheduled to end. In column C, describe what you currently know or predict is likely to happen to this income source (e.g. will it get bigger or smaller or will the availability of it change?). In column D, note any action that you need to take to secure or better manage this income source.

A Income	B Current position	C Prediction of trends	D Action needed

6 Setting the strategic direction

After clarifying what the organisation is for, taking stock of its development to date and obtaining a clearer financial picture, the planning process can now move on to setting a strategic direction.

Different definitions of strategy exist. In most definitions of organisational strategy the following elements are present:

- Making decisions about priorities.
- Linking current activities to future plans.
- Setting a direction or route for the organisation.
- Obtaining resources for the new direction.
- Managing change and setting objectives.

Most organisations (public, private or voluntary) were designed to allow vertical systems of command and control. People at the top of the organisation make important decisions and plans that are transmitted down the organisation by managers and supervisors to the people who should then carry them out.

In many organisations these levels do not link together at all well. Policy makers (senior managers and committee members) churn out policy papers, develop plans and demand change. People working at the operations level feel frustrated that new initiatives from the top and 'change for change's sake' get in the way of the real work of the organisation. Any sense of strategy that links policy to the day-to-day work is missing.

Other criticisms of this structure are that it militates against team work, slows down communication (as the structure gets bigger) and cuts off senior managers from seeing the impact of their work. Effective business planning and strategic management require good internal communication, good feedback and an ability to think about the whole of the organisation and not just specific departments.

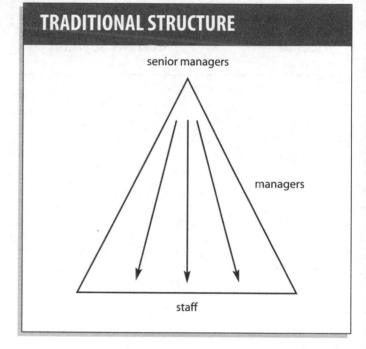

TRADITIONAL STRUCTURE

Often strategic management is about deciding what not to do as much as what to do. One charity director summed up this problem by referring to priorities. 'My organisation is brilliant at making priorities. We have hundreds, and they are all equally important. Every time I talk to my board or staff about the need to make priorities, I end up getting a few more.'

This chapter will look at four issues:

1 Establishing the assumptions behind the plan.
2 Identification of the organisation's limits.
3 Identifying strategic choices.
4 Agreeing and setting a strategic direction.

CASE STUDY

Same mission – different strategies

In 1986, health workers, community activists and people infected by HIV came together in a midlands town to create an organisation to do 'something about AIDS'. After a year of hard work raising the issue, running HIV awareness courses and providing practical support to people with HIV, the group held an away day to review progress. A key outcome of the day was a mission:

> 'To support people infected and affected by the disease and to overcome the ignorance and prejudice that surrounds it.'

The organisation's history could be described in three phases:

1 **Early days:** Driven by a feeling of impending crisis. Volunteer led. Fast growth. Self help.
2 **Early to late 1990s:** Appointment of staff to deliver a range of personal care, support and advocacy services to service users. Development of training programme delivered to key groups and communities.

3 **New phase:** Strong sense of change caused by the development of drug regimes that kept infected people alive, a reduced public profile about the disease and changing practices in funding. New direction was agreed that would focus much more on helping people to live with the disease, information about drug treatment and also take the education and prevention work into the mainstream

A further away day was held in 2001. At the end of this away day, one of the founding members commented how the original mission was still relevant, but the organisation's strategy for delivering it had had to change and respond to needs, demands and opportunities that existed.

This case shows how an organisation's mission should give it a longer-term sense of purpose and also how good strategy needs to be driven by being in touch with external developments and change.

● Establishing the assumptions behind the plan

Any planning process involves making some assumptions upon which planning can be based. Some commercial planners develop complex future-based scenarios to test out future possibilities. Other people rely on intelligent and informed guesswork. A business plan should set out the central assumptions behind it for the benefit of readers of the plan.

One approach is to list key assumptions under a series of headings:

KEY ASSUMPTIONS

Assumptions	Examples of assumptions made
Demand and needs	'That referrals will stay at the same rate over the next two years.' 'That demand for respite care will continue to rise.'
External developments	'That the local authorities will increasingly move towards spot or user based contracts.' 'That other agencies who work in this field will continue to charge a similar fee to ours.'
Internal developments	'That we will still be able to recruit, support and retain a volunteer team at its current level.' 'That staff turnover will remain at its current level.'
Financial	'That for the next two years increases in fee rates will meet inflation and pay awards.' 'That our fundraising income will rise by 5% each year for the next three years.'

Assumptions need to be credible, discussed openly and periodically checked.
The danger of operating according to an assumption that no longer applies is commonplace.

● Identification of the organisation's limits

All organisations have limits. Discussion of organisational strategy without reference to the organisation's limits is pointless daydreaming. Different sorts of limits exist. Some are fixed and some are more negotiable.

Possible limits include:

Physical
'Our current office could only cope with one more member of staff.'

Legal and constitutional
'Moving into this area of work could take us beyond our legal powers as a charity.'

Level of manageable risk
'To run this number of innovative and pioneering projects would be unacceptable to our trustees.'

Human
'Our current staff team are not skilled in this area of work.'

Resource
'To develop in such a way would stretch our management and communication systems.'

Financial
'To continue with this kind of funding will seriously harm our cash flow.'

Usually the most obvious limits are the resource or financial ones. However, it is interesting to look at how an organisation's traditions, practices and long-term commitments can also be a limiting factor.

Three questions are useful in reviewing the limiting factors:

1 How fixed is each limiting factor?
2 What creates the limiting factor?
3 What would we have to do to change it?

A useful exercise is to consider how the organisation would be different if it were to be created today. What would the organisation look like? What services would be provided? What would be the relationship to service users? It is interesting that many limiting factors are the direct product of the organisation's history. Some organisations have adopted a technique called zero base budgeting. Managers rebuild the budget for each activity as if they were starting it

again. The case for expenditure and staff time has to be justified against the organisation's strategy. It is interesting as a result of this exercise how many limiting factors are challenged, as resources previously committed are redirected to other priorities.

Exercise 12 on p.62 can be used to assess the limiting factors to your organisation's development.

Exercise 13 on p.63 will help you to analyse your organisation's ability to encourage innovation.

> *'Once enacted a budget becomes a precedent; the fact that something has been done once vastly increases the chances that it will be done again. Since only substantial departures from the previous year's budget are normally given intensive scrutiny, an item that remains unchanged will probably be carried along the following years as a matter of course…'*
> Wildavsky *The Politics of the Budgetary Process*

A LIMIT ON STRATEGY

The 'honeymoon period' in Kerry's new job as development manager for a charity for people with learning difficulties did not last long. She had been employed to research, design and set up new projects and initiatives. The charity desperately needed to improve its services and develop a commitment to user involvement. In her first few months, she developed proposals for three small projects. At first the reaction of her colleagues was very supportive.

Every six months managers met together for a planning day. The bulk of Kerry's first meeting was given over to consideration of her proposals. None of the managers present disagreed in principle with the proposals. However, each proposal was subject to detailed examination of the potential risk, the financial implications and the other costs. Kerry agreed to produce further reports and feasibility studies.

Three months after the strategy day, all of the projects were starting to 'slide off the drawing board'. However much extra information she produced, the projects were still being deferred.

Kerry fully understood that all new proposals needed rigorous review. However, she felt frustrated that many of the charity's current services were poor or in decline, but were never subject to any kind of review at all. Some were even at odds with the charity's recent statement of values and vision. Once projects had been established and were up and running, they carried on being allocated resources every year regardless. It was as if strategic management only applied to the consideration of new things and not to looking at current activities.

● Identifying strategic choices

All organisations have choices available to them. Doing nothing is one choice. Identifying choices and options for the future should be a participatory process that involves all individuals.

CASE STUDY

Identifying options by using scenarios

The Community Arts Team had reached a critical point in the agreement of its future strategy. In the ten years since it had been set up, it had developed a track record of running successful projects and programmes. Often the initiative or idea had come from spotting a pot of money and developing a project to fit with it. The team decided it needed a strategic plan to guide its future development.

Working with a consultant the team analysed its development to date. It reviewed past projects, looked at what other agencies were doing and identified key external trends and opportunities. The team soon realised that it had far too many ideas for how it could develop than it could possibly manage or resource. To move the plan forward the team put together a list of possible options and choices for how the team could develop over the next three to five years.

Community Arts Team – options and choices

SCENARIO 1
Aim to stay roughly as we are
This option assumed that the team would continue to be able to obtain funding and support to carry on with the same pattern of activities and projects.

SCENARIO 2
Focus on community regeneration
The team operated in an area scheduled for a major investment of government regeneration funds. This scenario would involve the team in working with the newly created regeneration partnership and using art forms to involve local people, encourage feedback and also to improve the urban environment.

SCENARIO 3
Become a community business
The team could develop a number of small- to medium-scale social businesses such as an internet café, an arts venue and an education and training programme that could operate on a proper business basis. Any profit made would be used to subsidise other activities.

SCENARIO 4
Reduce our focus
This option would mean that the team would only work with young people. This focus would give greater cohesion to the team and was based on a recognition that the team's greatest skills and competency were in working with younger people.

SCENARIO 5
Link up with a partner
The final option recognised that the team had developed a strong working link with a local theatre company. In many respects there were strong overlaps between their work. This option would involve much more shared working, joint bidding to run projects together and sharing of some resources. A longer-term possibility of merger would be explored.

The team presented each of the options to a special meeting of their management board. Each scenario was evaluated against the team's mission and the board's assessment of local need and possible funding. For some scenarios the board was able to do a simple cost/benefit analysis setting out possible pros and cons. Careful facilitation led the board away from trying to do all of them, to a position where a number of elements from three scenarios were combined together.

Participants felt that the process worked. Staff and board members felt positive that there was not just one possible way forward presented. The discussion on possible scenarios had to be informed by an understanding of the changing environment that the agency operated in.

A useful approach is to start by posing options for the future. Possibilities might include:

- Should we grow, stay the same or get smaller?
- What aspects of our work should we do more of or less of?
- What geographic areas should we do more in or less in?
- What style of work should we do more of or less of?
- Which client groups should we target?
- Should we become more specialist or more generalist?
- What alliances or relationships with others should we develop?

THE PROCESS INVOLVED IN SETTING A STRATEGIC DIRECTION

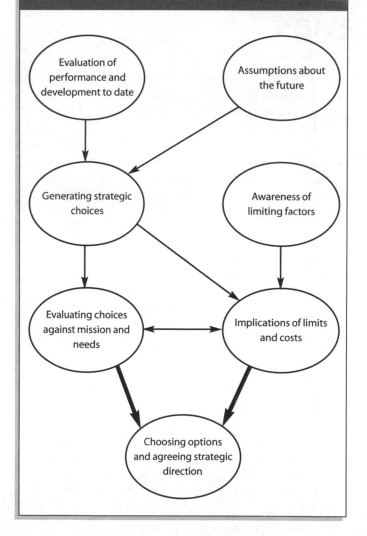

At this stage it is useful to bring into the discussion the users' perspective and the organisation mission. The focus of the direction needs to be on what the outside world needs and not just what feels comfortable for people in the organisation.

The list of options will probably be more than the organisation can deal with, so some sort of clear criteria are needed to evaluate possible choices. One agency worked

through the following four points in relation to each option that emerged:

- What is (or should be) distinctive about us as an organisation? Does this strategic option fit with our core mission and values?
- What are we effective at? What works? What do we do consistently well? Is our expertise best suited to this option?
- What are our priorities? What needs are most important to meet? Does this option fit with our priorities?
- Will this option be financially viable or, if not, is it important enough to subsidise? Will we be able to deliver?

Each option was examined according to the above criteria and graded accordingly. A number were quickly rejected, others were combined together and five were picked as the main driving force of the organisation.

● Agreeing and setting a strategic direction

Agreeing a strategic direction and aims involves constant reference back to the limiting factors and the overall mission. The process involves a continual movement between generating options, making priorities and working within the limiting factors.

At each stage the language of the plan changes. The mission statement will be hard to measure and act on. It is a statement of intent, not of specific action. The strategic aims need to indicate the clear direction and priority of the organisation for its immediate future. The objectives should be task centred and provide a measurable work plan for the organisation.

Experience in several organisations is that anything more than six to seven strategic aims leads to a plan (and an organisation) that is fragmented, confused and pulling in different directions.

Strategic aims need to:

- indicate a clear direction;
- be focused on intended outcomes;
- be integrated with other aims;
- be realistic and attainable.

Determining a future strategy often involves difficult decisions. Turning down someone's favourite project, deciding to withdraw from an area of work or shifting resources from one area to another will usually involve anxiety and conflict. As much attention will have to be paid to what the organisation is not going to do as to what it is.

Having established your aims, exercise 14 on p.64 will help you check that they amount to a clear direction for your organisation.

CASE STUDY

Moving from mission through strategy to objectives

The Eastside business advice agency was set up to help inner city residents explore the possibility of becoming self employed and creating small businesses. It is strongly committed to equal opportunities and full access to its services.

MISSION

'To provide high quality advice, training and support to emerging or newly created small businesses. The agency exists to support a viable and sustainable local economy. In carrying out this mission it will ensure that highest standards of quality assurance and equal opportunities apply throughout.'

STRATEGIC AIMS

The agency agreed four strategic aims to guide all of its work over the next two years:

- To continue to provide affordable and effective advice, counselling and information services to new or potential businesses.
- To provide a high quality training programme for business owners in three areas: management skills, marketing and quality assurance.
- To support cooperation between new businesses, encourage marketing of inner city businesses and identify new business opportunities.
- To investigate and pilot ways of supporting businesses facing insolvency.

SPECIFIC OBJECTIVES

For aim 3, 'To support cooperation between new businesses, encourage marketing of inner city businesses and identify new business opportunities', there are six objectives:

- To encourage three inner city business networks through monthly breakfast seminars and quarterly business forums. The forums should aim to attract 150 participants in total. (100 hours)
- To organise four self-financing business advertisement campaigns promoting local business. (30 hours)
- To create a women's business forum that will have a minimum of 20 participants and be able to be self managing. (60 hours, to be implemented by February)
- To organise an inner city business exhibition, target attendance 400 people. (300 hours, planned date in October, budget: £12,000)
- To have developed and implemented a strategy to raise funds for a food purchasing and distribution cooperative. (75 hours, first report to January management committee)
- To participate in the management committee of the electronic village steering group. (45 hours)

The objectives were produced by the relevant team member. They estimated how much time they would spend on each item as an indicator of priorities. The objectives became the work plan for each staff member.

Once the strategic aims have been agreed, objectives need to be established for each area. A well used mnemonic for writing objectives is SMART.

Specific
Measurable
Attainable
Realistic
Timed

There is a danger that senior managers will write too much of the plan. Clearly, trustees and managers have the responsibility for the mission and agreeing the strategic aims, but if they involve themselves in the detail of the operational objectives then the plan will never properly become the property of the organisation. One agency adopted a four-stage approach to agreeing its strategy.

First a joint staff and management committee meeting agreed a mission statement. After considerable discussion the management committee agreed five aims. Each aim was then delegated to an appropriate staff group who reviewed their activities and worked out a detailed work plan within the boundary set by the core aims. The management committee then agreed all of the work objectives.

Many business plans use a format of a plan that cascades through different levels:

FORMAT OF A PLAN

The mission	The purpose and values statement.
↓	
Strategic aims	A limited number of priorities. A route for the organisation to follow.
↓ ↓ ↓	
Objectives	Costed, detailed and timed action plans for each strategic aim.

● Ten ways in which funding can distort your organisation!

It is important to ensure that although the need for funding and income generation is part of the strategic process, it does not dominate or distort it. Here are ten ways in which the wrong kind of funding can distort your organisation's strategy and even damage the organisation.

1   It's all short-termism

Year-to-year funding scrambles make long-term planning hard. The organisation lacks security and finds it hard to recruit and retain staff. A lot of work goes into starting projects and activities, but an absence of any long-term funding means that they never really deliver their potential.

2   Capital rich – revenue poor

Going for a capital project such as new building can create a major focus for fundraising effort. Often in the enthusiasm to raise the capital amount the annual running costs are underestimated or overlooked.

3   No-one pays for the centre

Many funding bodies are keen to fund projects and specific programmes rather than simply to grant aid an organisation. This can create an organisational imbalance – new work is developed, but the organisation's infrastructure and management systems are not sufficient to support and service them.

4   Cash flow kills

It is not just how much you get from a funder but it is also when you get it. Having to chase money and deal with uneven patterns of income and expenditure (such as spending most of the money in the first half of the year, but not being paid until the third quarter) can test an organisation's management and financial capacity.

5   Strings attached

Sometimes funders will attach restrictions to how a fund can be spent, or earmark it for a particular purpose. A problem occurs if meeting such directions distorts the work of the organisation. Workers at a youth development agency noted that their focus was being directed to work with 18–24-year-olds, as that group was seen as a priority by funders. Other groups that the agency considered a priority were being ignored.

6   They won't last for ever

Most capital purchases (buildings, equipment, vehicles) will need either replacing with new ones or at the very least repairing and upgrading. They usually depreciate in value.

7   Fast growth

Growth can be hard to manage. Rapid expansion of an organisation's services and activities needs to be matched with a growth in the organisation's management capacity and ability.

8   Uneven growth

Sometimes one aspect of an organisation's work becomes attractive to funders. Money starts to pour into it. It radiates success and prestige. It is tempting to focus all energy and effort into it. This can cause problems for other parts of the organisation. Care is needed to ensure that long-term work is not lost because a particular area of work has become 'flavour of the month'.

9   High management costs

Some forms of funding have high transaction costs. Funders expect regular monitoring reports, performance measures, audit returns and other management tasks. The cost and time of such tasks needs to be recognised and budgeted for.

10   Didn't want to be here

Often funding can take you down a path to somewhere that you did not want to go. Over a three-year period a community regeneration project noticed its work changing from community development to running vocational training courses. The project leader commented, 'A pot of money became available to open up access routes back to college – we applied for it and were successful. Although some good work has been done, it has shifted our focus, changed our culture and our relationship to our users – we never wanted to be a mini college.'

● Managing it

Operate short term – think long term

The limitations and frustrations of short-term funding can make longer-term strategic thinking feel impossible. However, to avoid crisis management it is important to develop a longer-term view, both of financial issues and of the longer-term strategic development of the organisation. A good business planning process should take the longer view and help the organisation prepare a series of contingencies and possible longer-term plans.

Use the business plan

The business plan can be used as a valuable tool to explain the financial basis of the organisation, alert people to key risks, show that the organisation is thinking strategically and also to make the case for a sound organisational infrastructure.

Influence funders

Involving funders in the planning process can help them to understand the financial realities of the organisation and to see how their possible investment can best be made.

Do not be led by funding alone

As organisations grow there is a tendency to hive off fundraising and create a separate fundraising function. Often fundraisers can see opportunities for future funding or feel that they would be more successful if the organisation developed in a particular way. This can lead to compartmental thinking or even conflict between fundraisers and other staff. It is important that fundraisers are involved in the whole planning process and not simply given a target to meet at the end of the process. They need to understand the whole picture. Equally the organisation needs to decide what it wants to do and then look for funding.

▼ **Exercise 12**

WHAT'S THE LIMIT?

Think about your organisation. What are the limiting factors to its growth and development?

Limiting factor	How fixed is it?	Strategies to overcome it

▼ **Exercise 13**

WHEN DID YOU LAST HAVE A NEW IDEA?

Many voluntary organisations pride themselves on being innovative. They see themselves as being dynamic and challenging. What is the reality?

One worker in a national organisation described her organisation's approach to new ideas as:

> 'If someone has an idea that they want to push for, they have to be prepared to run an obstacle course of working groups, consultation meetings and discussion papers. It will take months. Any plan that emerges (and quite a few don't), will have had any inventive or creative element drained out of it.'

Managing new ideas and creating innovation tests many organisations. The following exercise aims to help you to evaluate the capacity of your organisation to be innovative and ensure that the plan does have a creative element.

List any new or dynamic ideas or initiatives that have got off the drawing board in your organisation in the past two years.

What are the factors that encourage innovation in the organisation?

What are the factors that discourage innovation in the organisation?

What does the organisation do to encourage new ideas?

(Possible examples could include having a research and development budget, evaluating current services, encouraging project teams etc.)

How could this be improved?

What happens when new ideas or innovative projects go wrong?

What is the balance in the plan between ongoing work and new work?

How can new ideas, creative strategies and innovative work be encouraged in the planning process?

▼ **Exercise 14**

HOW CLEAR IS THE DIRECTION?

This exercise is useful to attempt after the main strategic aims of the organisation have been agreed. If the answers are uncertain or vague then it may mean that the direction agreed is not decisive enough.

If the strategic aims are successfully implemented…

What will be different about the organisation?

> Will it:
> • be bigger or smaller?
> • be doing more things or fewer things?
> • have the same users or different ones?
> • be generalist or targeted?
> • be working in the same ways or different ways?

What will be the key differences if this strategy is implemented?

Try to describe the significant changes of the new direction as if you were writing a newspaper headline.

What will still be the same?

What will the organisation do more and less of?

> More of:

> Less of:

7 Establishing credibility

A business plan needs to make the case for an organisation. It needs to establish confidence in the minds of potential backers that the organisation is competent enough to successfully manage the plan. A manager of a trust that requires business plans as part of its application process commented, 'The idea behind the plan may well be brilliant. But we need to know that it has the people and systems in place to implement it. We look to the business plan to convince us that the organisation has a track record and that the key personnel involved are experienced in similar activities.'

The business plan can demonstrate this in four ways:

1 Providing evidence that the organisation has a history of sound practice and good management.
2 Establishing that the organisation has in place systems and structures which are appropriate to the scale and demands of the plan.
3 Showing that the organisation has within it a core of personnel with sufficient skills to implement the plan.
4 Proving that in the case of new initiatives, sufficient feasibility work on the plans has been carried out.

Many voluntary organisations seem reluctant or unwilling to positively record or market their own expertise, skills and competence. The process of collecting this information can have some very useful side effects. It can put them in a much stronger position with funders and purchasers, and it can also increase the organisation's own confidence in itself.

For smaller organisations or newer projects the plan might need to show that there are sufficient support systems around it to help it.

● Collecting evidence

The following six points are possible sources of evidence that an organisation has a good track record:

1 Financial records. Previous accounts and audits could show that the organisation has properly managed its financial affairs in the past.

2 External evaluations. Recorded evaluation studies could indicate strengths of the organisation.
3 Feedback from users. Client reaction, client follow up and repeat work could indicate that the organisation is capable of providing a service that people want.
4 Third party references. Sponsorship from eminent people could establish credibility. A health group used backing from medical consultants in its business plan to establish credibility with health purchasers.
5 Client list. A list of current or past organisational clients or partners could indicate credibility, particularly if client organisations agreed to act as referees.
6 Evidence of successful work. Press cuttings, case studies and case follow-ups might create a positive feel about the organisation.

● Demonstrating organisational competence

A business plan needs to show that the organisation has in place the systems and processes necessary to properly manage the plan. The following list sets out nine areas of evidence that can help to show your organisation is sound, effective and well managed.

1 Evidence of good organisational practice

The existence of an equal opportunities policy, complaints procedure, staff development policies and other statements might show that, on paper at least, the organisation is clear about how it should work.

2 A quality assurance policy

Quality assurance is about three things: finding out from users what is important about how the service operates; establishing minimum quality standards that indicate what can be expected from a service; and ensuring that the organisation consistently meets the standards. A quality assurance policy should set out key standards and indicate how they will be monitored and improved.

Many organisations have now developed their own quality standards setting out minimum levels of practice and expectations. Some national networks have also produced national standards of best practice for local groups to follow. Charities Evaluation Services has produced a self-managed quality assurance framework called Pquasso – specifically for smaller voluntary sector organisations. It covers sixteen quality areas and can help staff and management committees identify what the organisation is doing well and what it needs to improve.

3   An external award of formal quality assurance certification

There are now various quality assurance systems whereby an organisation contracts with and usually pays for an independent inspector to carry out an audit of practice. In some industries the award of the British quality standard, IS9000, is an almost mandatory requirement. Some contracts can only be awarded to companies with IS9000 accreditation. All IS9000 indicates is that the management practices used to manage a system are rigorous and comprehensive enough to satisfy an external audit. It does not comment on the benefit to users of the service being provided or the relevance of the standards set. Another common external standard is Investors In People (IIP) which is awarded after an external review of an organisation's staff training and development policies.

There are also some sector-specific assurance systems such as the Community Legal Service's quality mark.

4   Membership of a national organisation

Many smaller organisations or projects could point to their membership of a national organisation as evidence of having back-up services such as training, specialist advice and information. The national organisation might also provide some quality assurance function.

5   Successful reviews, audits and inspections

Evidence of successful regular audits or inspections by creditable external inspectors or funding bodies might make other potential backers or funders feel confident about the organisation.

6   Evidence of sound management practice

The plan might want to show that the organisation has people working in it, around it (e.g. on its management committee) or advising it (as consultants or other experts) who have the skills and experience to ensure that the plan can be delivered.

7   Successful delivery of other activities and projects

It is worthwhile to list previous projects and activities that the organisation has successfully delivered to show that it has a good track record in this respect.

8   Evidence of staff development and training

Proof of a commitment to staff development can be shown by percentage of turnover spent on staff development, or average number of days that staff spent on training and development activities, or by the operation of effective personnel practices such as appraisal or supervision sessions.

9   User feedback

Evidence of feedback from users, preferably collected by an independent third party, can show that a service works well and meets expectation.

All of this information should be presented in brief summary form – if readers want to know more they can ask for it.

● Competence of key people

Some business plans include the outline curriculum vitae of all the management team members. This may be going into too much detail, but the following information might help convince backers that the organisation has within it sufficient skilled people:

- Background details and experience of key staff.
- Background details and experience of management committee and trustees.
- Names of external advisers, accountants, solicitors and specialist consultants.
- Relevant qualified staff.
- Staff development policies.

CASE STUDY

Proving credibility

The Family in Crisis charity was a new group set up by parents and some professionals to provide counselling, support and help to families in times of turmoil and stress. Initially the group worked with a network of volunteers coordinated by a worker paid for by a trust. However, changes in community care prompted the committee to approach the Health Authority to discuss how they might work together and the possibilities of financial support.

The first discussion with the Health Authority was positive. The charity's services fitted in extremely well with several elements of the community care plan and with current priorities. The authority asked for a business plan so that they could consider it further.

The draft business plan followed a format set out in a high street bank's new business guide. The section asking them to 'list the relevant experience of key personnel' was initially hard. The Heath Authority officer had commented that it was of concern to them that all 'potential providers were professional'. At first this was seen by the committee as a weakness as they were 'only volunteers'. Surely the criteria favoured businesses or statutory organisations and put a small voluntary organisation at a disadvantage?

The committee carried out a mapping exercise to list the various skills they had. Amongst the committee's membership were a finance manager in a private company, a retired headteacher, a legal executive and a woman who had set up and ran a successful small business. The group had within it significant management expertise, but, perhaps as importantly, was their combined local knowledge, contacts and personal experience of living with and surviving family crisis.

The charity also had around it a network of people who had during different stages of the charity's history provided help and support. They included two doctors, an assistant director of social services and a psychotherapist. These individuals agreed to form an advisory panel to the charity, separate from the management structure, that would advise the management committee and ensure a quality service.

Despite initial doubts, it was now clear that for the size of the organisation the charity had within or around it considerable skills and experience.

● Proving that a new project is feasible

Many small businesses (and possibly some voluntary projects) fail because the individuals who start up are so full of passion for their project that it gets in the way of any genuine feasibility study. The commitment to the vision and dream becomes so important that questions such as whether it will work and who will pay for it are seen as negative and diversionary. For a new project the business plan needs to set out:

■ How the need for it has been identified.

■ What the need is.

■ What support there is for the project.

■ How the proposed project will meet the need.

■ What the start-up costs will be.

■ How the project will be researched and tested.

Evidence should be included to show that possible pitfalls and alternatives have been explored. A useful exercise is to try to predict all of the potential questions and challenges there will be to the project and then assemble evidence to answer them. It is also useful in discussing a project's feasibility to identify in the business plan potential risks involved in the project and suggest how that risk can best be managed. It is better to acknowledge a risk first and deal with it than to let someone else identify it as an undisclosed weakness.

The following exercise gives you the chance to set out the evidence which proves your plan's viability.

▼ **Exercise 15**

PROVING YOUR TRACK RECORD

A business plan should show that the organisation is capable of achieving its plan. It will need to show evidence that the organisation or the key people within it have the competence and experience to manage the plan successfully.

What evidence do you have of the following elements?

Sound financial management

Effective response to needs

A consistent quality of service

Good management practice

What other strengths or organisational assets need highlighting in the plan?

8 Presenting the business plan

Putting the business plan on paper is an important task. The document needs to be concise, present the plans for the organisation and convince people that the organisation is credible. The plan has to be of use both externally and internally.

A business plan needs to give an honest appraisal of an organisation's development to date. It should note weaknesses and setbacks, as well as strengths and achievements. Some of the most effective plans are the ones that give a full picture of an organisation, and also clearly indicate what action management will be taking to improve performance where it has been lacking.

There is sometimes a problem with releasing a business plan that could be of value to a competitor. A manager of a training centre experienced this problem when required to produce a business plan for a tender to manage a government training programme. She explained that, 'Our business plan contained details of how we cost our work, staffing levels and management arrangements. This information represented the product of years of work of trying to get the service right. We have always worked in a very open way, but I would be unhappy if some of the agencies we now compete with had sight of it. We did submit it, but on the condition that its circulation was restricted.'

The business plan itself followed a format similar to the one set out in this chapter. It was made available to funders and purchasers, who could request any further information. The one-page executive summary was attached to the business plan as a covering document and also used in presentations about the organisation. It was particularly useful for dealing with politicians who had little time to read the full document and only really needed to know the overall direction. The summary document was a freely available publication circulated to the public. The action plan was described by one staff member as a 'management bible' and regularly used by staff working to the business plan.

The executive summary is particularly important. It is easy to get lost in the detail of the plan itself. It is important to remember that many potential backers use the summary, or in its absence a two-minute glance through the full document, to get 'a feel of the plan'. This first impression can often greatly influence future considerations. The executive summary should highlight the main features of the organisation, set out its direction and make clear what is expected from others.

Exercise 16 on p.73 provides an opportunity to focus on the key messages of your plan.

CORE DOCUMENTS

It is often helpful to produce a core document with three additional documents related to it:

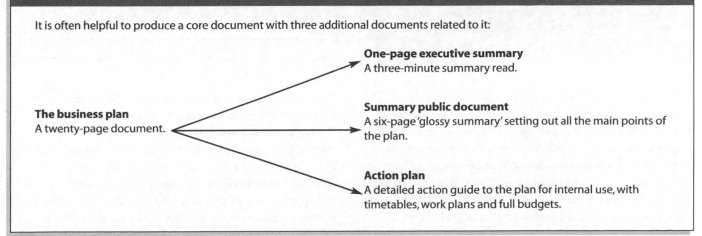

The business plan
A twenty-page document.

One-page executive summary
A three-minute summary read.

Summary public document
A six-page 'glossy summary' setting out all the main points of the plan.

Action plan
A detailed action guide to the plan for internal use, with timetables, work plans and full budgets.

EXAMPLE OF A ONE-PAGE EXECUTIVE SUMMARY

Eastside Business Agency

The agency is a registered charity and established as a company limited by guarantee. Established in 1987, it operates in the east side of the city, an area of declining employment, high adult unemployment and social deprivation. The agency's mission is as follows:

'The agency exists to support a viable and sustainable local economy. It does this by providing high quality advice, training and support to emerging or newly created small businesses. In carrying out this mission it will ensure that the highest standards of quality and equal opportunities apply throughout.'

The agency's seven-strong staff team provides initial advice for those considering self employment, practical help with business start-ups, training and consultancy, joint marketing and continued contact with new businesses in their first three years of operation. We deal with an average of 45 new or potential new businesses at any one time. A recent evaluation shows that the agency has helped to create 126 new businesses in Eastside employing nearly 300 people. 39% of our clients are from the Black and Asian communities.

The agency has developed successful partnerships and funding arrangements with the City Council, the Training and Enterprise Council and the Eastside Regeneration Partnership. One of the high points of last year was the award of the Investors In People standard as a recognition of our commitment to staff development.

This two-year business plan has two central themes – the consolidation of the agency's work and the development of new services to help established businesses survive the difficult trading climate.

The plan puts forward four strategic aims. The first two will consolidate our existing advice, counselling and information services and continue our popular business training programme. Our third aim is to encourage practical cooperation and joint marketing of existing businesses. Our fourth aim is to pilot new ways of providing assistance to businesses approaching or facing insolvency. This is a new area of work for the agency and is in response to growing enquiries from our clients.

The plan sets out how this strategy can be achieved with continued support from our current partners. The strategy includes the gradual closure of our grants advisory service and the creation of a new post of marketing support manager.

The organisation is now an established and proven agency working within the inner city. This plan sets out a two-year future for its continued success.

Careful thought needs to be given to the style and format of the business plan itself. It is useful to list the main messages (no more than five) that you want the plan to convey and organise the rest of the information and evidence around them. Some business plans suffer from being written by people who are so close to the organisation that they cannot see it as an outsider would. Obvious pieces of information are forgotten, jargon is used and assumptions made. It is worthwhile to get someone who is detached from the organisation to read it through or to edit it.

● A rolling plan

How long can you write a plan for? This is an obvious question which is often asked. A business plan needs to be future based, but accurate planning is difficult to the point of impossible when key factors such as the level of funding are only known in the short term.

One useful solution to this problem is to see the business plan as a rolling plan. In a rolling plan an overall purpose and strategy are set for, say, three years, but the detailed work plan and operating budget are updated on an annual basis. For example, an agency working on the economic and social regeneration of an estate took the view that its mission was a long-term statement of aims and goals. The mission was an end to work to. The goal set out in the strategy would take at least two to three years to deliver. The third level of planning – work plans and budgets – could be updated on an annual basis to reflect circumstances, resources available and local needs. The business planning process therefore became a rolling process whereby the operational plan was reviewed, developed and agreed annually.

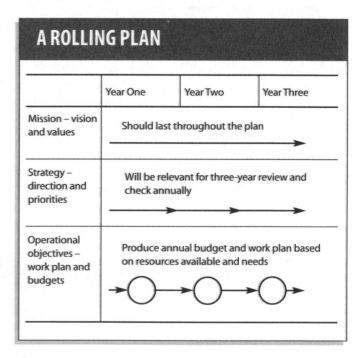

A ROLLING PLAN

	Year One	Year Two	Year Three
Mission – vision and values	Should last throughout the plan		
Strategy – direction and priorities	Will be relevant for three-year review and check annually		
Operational objectives – work plan and budgets	Produce annual budget and work plan based on resources available and needs		

The agency's three-year business plan outlines mission and strategy and then has attached to it as an appendix the current year's operational plan and budget. At the start of every year the agency's staff and management board review the strategy, agree a work plan based on the strategy and agree an annual budget. The agency's coordinator feels that this approach is realistic, keeps the plan alive and is based on having a planning process rather than a fixed document.

● Eight points about writing the plan

1 It is harder to write a short document than a long one. After about fifteen pages it is probable that there will be so much detail that the main direction will be lost.

2 Do not assume that people understand what the organisation does or what the needs of its users are. This can even apply to people who have been donating income for years.

3 Use summaries and action points to create a feeling of direction and purpose.

4 Use some of the exercises used in this book, such as the SWOT analysis and portfolio matrix to show your analysis and thinking.

5 Think carefully about how to present financial information. Make sure that the assumptions behind future forecasts are stated.

6 Use graphs and charts to explain information, but check that the message is not distorted by them.

7 Keep the style and language of the document active and task centred. It should be clear and specific not vague and ambiguous.

8 Get someone external to the organisation to read it through and ask them to identify any unclear thinking, unproven assumptions or the use of jargon.

Exercise 17 on p.74 gives you a format for writing your business plan.

THE STRUCTURE OF A BUSINESS PLAN

Section	Content
An 'executive summary'	Brief outline of mission, values and context. It should highlight the proposed direction, key benefits and make the case for the organisation. A one-page three-minute read.
Introduction and mission	The mission statement in full. Explanation of purpose and duration of the plan.
The organisation's background	A brief history of the organisation. Its legal status and registered office. You need to include basic and factual information to help readers get a picture of your organisation: • Status of the organisation: legal status, relationship to any parent organisation. • Scale of operation: where you work, what you do and who with. • Size of the operation: number of projects, staff and turnover.
A summary review	A short review of the organisation to date. Stress strengths, achievements and external recognition to date. Readers may expect to see some honest appraisal of weaknesses. A SWOT analysis is often used to display this information.
Future trends	An outline of how the organisation sees its future environment developing. Refer to likely needs of users. The plan needs to show that thought has been given to likely external developments.
Strategic direction	What assumptions underpin the chosen direction? What will be the main direction of the organisation's work? What will be its main priorities? What will be different?
Strategic aims	Statement of aims for the medium term. The specific objectives for each aim could be listed or a brief summary of them given.
Implications	Areas of work that will be dropped or phased out should be noted. Organisational, legal or any other key implications should be listed here.
Financial implications	How will the plan be funded? Income and expenditure projections for first year and estimates for following years. Listing of financial assumptions behind the plan. Statement of key financial policy (e.g. pricing policy) and evidence of efficient management (e.g. cash flow forecast).
Track record of the organisation	Making the case for the organisation. Showing that it has the management competence and experience necessary to manage the plan. The past experience of the organisation and its key personnel could be listed. A list of critical success factors.
Immediate action plan	Timed action for the first steps in the plan.

● After the plan … more planning

The managers of Hillgate Care recognised that their newly agreed business plan would require radical change for the charity. The charity was well established and had provided care and support schemes for a range of adults with learning disabilities. The new plan was based on a recognition that the organisation needed to change, embrace best practice and also follow up opportunities to expand into neighbouring local authorities. The plan had four main strategic priorities:

- To encourage and support the involvement and participation of the service users throughout.
- To broaden the income base by expanding into neighbouring local authorities.
- To develop a community business to create employment for some users.
- To develop a home support service to support some users living independently.

The management team agreed to set up three implementation groups to draw up action plans and lead the work. The three groups were:

● *A business/service development group*

This group was charged with developing a business case for each new service and for setting up a marketing campaign to develop new business.

● *A staff development group*

The team recognised that the plan would require new skills in the organisation. This group was given the responsibility of setting up a staff training programme focused on user involvement and also a programme for staff moving from a centre to an outreach role.

● *An organisation group*

The organisation group was given the responsibility of ensuring that the organisation's infrastructure could cope with growth. The group developed an action plan to look at what new systems and processes would be needed to support expansion.

All of the groups were established as fixed-term projects for three months. Staff appointed to each group were asked to give a minimum of three days and a maximum of six days to work on the group. Each group was asked to prepare an action plan for their work which was approved by the management committee. The action plans were structured around the following six key issues.

STRUCTURE FOR AN ACTION PLAN

Success criteria	How will we judge success? What is the overall goal?
Key activities	An outline of the programme of work needed
Work plan	A timed programme of the key tasks, events and activities
Resource need	A statement of financial, human and other resources needed to accomplish the plan
Milestones	A plan setting out key review dates
Responsibility	Named lead responsibility for implementing the plan

The charity's director commented that she had learnt three things as a result of the process:

1 The importance of moving from strategy to detail
'There is a danger that planning gets stuck at the level of mission and overall strategy. The implementation planning is about making it real and agreeing the first steps in getting it moving.'

2 The value of involving staff in planning implementation
'By involving staff from across the organisation in drawing up the implementation plans we created real communication and encouraged people to feel that they were involved and owned the plan.'

3 Things do not happen unless a responsibility is allocated
'We went through every line of the plan and made sure that an individual was responsible for ensuring that action happened on every commitment and target. Attaching a name to a plan and ensuring that progress is checked makes it real.'

You may wish to use exercise 18 on p.76 to evaluate the effectiveness of the different aspects of your plan.

▼ Exercise 16

THE ELEVATOR TEST

An exercise borrowed from commercial venture capitalists is a simple and challenging way of testing how clear you are about the main messages of your business plan.

Imagine that you are visiting a potential funder at their office to talk over your new business plan. At the reception you press the button to summon the lift. As you wait for the lift you are joined by the Chief Executive of the funding body. The Chief Executive has met you before and asks why you are visiting their organisation. You explain that you are dropping off a copy of your new business plan, in the hope that it might lead to funding.

The lift arrives and you both enter it. The Chief Executive comments that she will probably not have time to read your plan and asks you what are the main messages of your business plan and why should they back it.

It will take 3–4 minutes for the lift journey. You are unlikely to get another chance to talk directly to the Chief Executive again. What would you say?

Review

How easy was it to identify the main messages?
What are the main messages that you want readers of the plan to remember?
How well does the plan present them and highlight them?

▼ Exercise 17

PUTTING THE PLAN ON PAPER

This template sets out a format for the business plan. It follows a logical format:

- It describes the organisation as it is now.
- It sets out an appraisal of the organisation as it stands and also highlights the main issues and trends taking place in the organisation's external environment.
- It outlines the organisation's future strategy and key priorities

- It sets out what resources will be needed to deliver the strategy
- It concludes by showing that the organisation has the internal capacity and experience to properly manage resources and deliver the plan.

Use the space after each section to make a note of your answers to, or thoughts about, the key points given.

Section 1 An 'executive summary'	**Key points** What are the main points (no more than five) that you want readers to remember about the plan?

Section 2 Introduction and mission	**Key points** Can you sum up the organisation's purpose and key values in no more than forty words?

Section 3 The organisation's background	**Key points** What background information about the organisation do readers need to know to understand the plan?

Section 4 A summary review	**Key points** Sum up the organisation's record to date. Avoid going into too much detail.

Section 5 Future trends	**Key points** Set out the bigger picture. What will the organisation's future environment look like – users profile, trends, needs and opportunities.

Section 6 Strategic direction	**Key points** What assumptions are you making about the future? What will be the organisation's main direction for the next period?

Section 7 Strategic aims	**Key points** Statement of core aims for the organisation as a whole – no more than six key aims. Specific objectives on how each aim will be implemented.

Section 8 Implications	**Key points** To meet this plan what will you have to do differently? What changes in how the organisation currently works will have to be managed?

Section 9 Financial implications	**Key points** How will the plan be funded? Financial projections and estimates. Summary of financial policy.

Section 10 Track record of the organisation	**Key points** Evidence that the organisation is capable of meeting the plan. What are your critical success factors?

Section 11 Immediate action plan	**Key points** Detailed implementation plan for the first steps.

▼ Exercise 18

EVALUATING YOUR PLAN

Does the plan create a clear sense of purpose or mission that all of the organisation can work towards?

Action Points

_____

_____

Are all of the strategic aims and detailed objectives in the plan consistent with the mission?

Action Points

_____

_____

Are you confident that you have adequately gathered information about possible external events, trends and possibilities that will affect your organisations future?

Action Points

_____

_____

On a continuum ranging from 'bleakly pessimistic' to 'wildly optimistic', evaluate the main decisions and aims within the plan.

Bleakly pessimistic	Wildly optimistic

Do any of these decisions and aims cause you concern?

Action Points

_____

_____

On a continuum ranging from 'wild guess' to 'guaranteed forecast', evaluate the main forecasts and projections in the plan.

Wild guess	Guaranteed forecast

Do any of these forecasts and projections cause you concern?

Action Points

_____

_____

On a continuum of 'mission impossible' to 'will be easy to achieve', evaluate the specific objectives and work commitments set out in the plan.

mission impossible	will be easy to achieve

Do any of these specific objectives and work commitments cause you concern?

Action Points

_____

_____

List the five main messages that you would like readers of the plan to retain:

1 How clearly does the plan convey these points?
2 How will you know if the plan has worked?
3 What feedback and monitoring systems will you use?
4 What will be the first steps after agreeing the plan?
5 What will be the plan's immediate action plan?

_____

9 Managing the plan
Putting it into practice

As described in the introduction to this book, many organisations invest time in the planning process, produce a business plan and then file it away. It is forgotten until it has to be worked on again. The plan remains a paper document that gathers dust on the shelf. Three reasons might contribute to this:

1 The plan never really dealt with the realities of the organisation. It is all about how people would like it to be in a perfect world.
2 The process of putting the plan together never engaged people who need to implement it. The managers or external consultants who drove the planning process never created a feeling of ownership throughout the organisation.
3 The plan itself is fine, but managers do not have either the time or the skill to manage the changes involved.

The first two issues are dealt with earlier in this book. This chapter will focus on the processes involved in overcoming the third obstacle. It deals with five questions:

1 How to identify a management focus to implement the plan.
2 How to make the plan a relevant and living document for everyone in the organisation.
3 How to monitor, measure and ensure that the assumptions behind the plan are still relevant.
4 How to manage changes involved in the plan.
5 What is meant by strategic management.

The chapter is rounded off with a further series of exercises designed to help you focus on managing your business plan.

● Identifying a management focus

Often the hardest part of managing is for the manager to know where to exert limited time, energy and effort.

One established technique is to identify those factors that managers need to focus on if they are to be successful. These factors are known as critical success factors. They are the keys to the successful implementation and completion of the business plan. They are the things that the organisation believes it has to get right if it is to meet the plan.

Success factors are usually a mixture of 'hard' elements (things that are tangible and easy to measure, such as outputs) and 'softer' issues (such as processes, working culture and styles of work).

It is important to limit the number of factors. Too many will lead to a lack of management focus. Once agreed, managers should work out exactly what they need to do to work on each issue and draw up clear and measurable action plans for each factor.

One management team attempted to draw up a list of critical success factors for their work. The final statement came from a session in which managers listed the things that they needed to change about how they managed, the things that they needed to improve and, importantly, the things that they needed to keep doing well. The final list was arrived at after some considerable negotiation within the management team. Responsibility for leading particular items were allocated to team members and review dates set. The critical success factors became the agenda for the management team for the coming year.

CASE STUDY

Developing critical success factors

The Halfway project provides practical help and supported accommodation to people with learning difficulties. It employs 38 staff and operates in four local authority areas.

After reconsidering its mission, and agreeing a strategic direction and priorities, it set about identifying the key elements that it would need to work on to get from its current position to the intended one set out in the business plan.

After identifying specific aims for the organisation (e.g. to develop a new service in a particular location), it also agreed eight factors that managers would need to work on to manage the successful completion of its aims and objectives. It would have been possible to have a much longer list. However, the team felt that it was better to focus all its effort on the eight points rather than to try to cope with a longer list.

The factors were:

1 Much better communication between the main office and projects. Must feel that we are all part of one organisation. More attention to teamwork.
2 Need to reduce paperwork and duplication of systems. Enhanced use new of technology.
3 Better financial management system. We need to know exactly what each activity or project costs and have better control of costs in order to properly negotiate contracts.
4 More attention to securing the long-term commitment of our current individual and corporate donors. Persuading existing donors to give regularly and feel a strong loyalty link with us.
5 Our name, image and identity need reviewing. Need for crisper, more modern and better understood public image.
6 Need to develop our skills and expertise in marketing, and in negotiating and costing service agreements and contracts.
7 Must develop a commitment to innovation, experimentation and new work. Innovation must be encouraged and rewarded.
8 Need for the two senior managers to spend more time on the strategic development of the organisation and less on detailed 'micro-managing'.

● Making the plan a relevant and living document

Experience in many organisations suggests that the sooner people affected by a plan are involved in contributing to it, the more likely it is that they will feel committed to its implementation. Even if early involvement has been achieved, there is still a need to market and explain the plan internally to staff (existing and new staff), volunteers and supporters. Some national charities have developed an internal communication procedure to explain their mission and direction to staff as, often, people working within a part of the organisation fail to see the bigger picture of their work.

The following four examples show how some organisations have tried to explain and relate their business plan to individual employees.

■ One national charity ensured that each member of staff received a copy of the business plan and had a meeting with their line manager. The meeting identified possible implications of the plan for their work, drew up an action plan for them and discussed future priorities.

■ A housing association used the direction set out in its business plan as an input into a training needs analysis. The business plan identified a strategy that involved negotiating private finance for projects and operating in a competitive market. Consequently, the training needs analysis identified negotiating and marketing skills as important skill gaps within the organisation.

■ One agency included in its staff appraisal scheme what contribution managers had made to meeting the business plan. It identified potential problems and helped managers focus their efforts.

■ One charity produced a special staff newsletter explaining the business plan in detail. This was followed up by visits to every unit by a senior manager to discuss the plan in detail.

● Monitoring, measuring and ensuring that the assumptions behind the plan are still relevant

Possibly the best test of the strategic aims and objectives is 'Can they be easily measured and monitored?' Often when something is hard to measure, it reveals that the objective for it is not clear. Several different types of measures are available:

DIFFERENT TYPES OF MEASURES

Progress measures	Reporting on specific work to date
Volume or output measures	Reporting on the number using a service
	Occupancy rate or number of activities completed
Reaction measures	Feedback from users
Impact measures	Reports on the immediate benefits of the output
Outcome measures	Longer-term benefits and results

The measures for the strategic aims should be mainly impact and outcome measures. They should focus on what was achieved, what needs were met and what longer-term benefits were identified. The objective measures are likely to be progress, output/volume or reaction measures.

Monitoring the parts of the plan

Business plans needs milestones. A number of measures should be established to check progress, identify problems early and enable action. The chart below sets out some of the things that could be monitored and suggests a possible time scale. The time scale would need to be fixed to take into account the particular circumstances of the organisation. For example, an organisation managing several high-risk projects to a tight budget might require more frequent reports. There is a blank chart on p.87 for you to use.

MONITORING THE PLAN

Issue	Monitor
Mission	Very occasionally, every two to three years.
Are the assumptions in the plan still valid?	Every six months or when deemed necessary.
Are the strategic aims still the right ones?	At least annually.
Progress/outcome of each aim	Written report, produced quarterly or every six months.
Progress report on each objective	Monthly or quarterly written report.
Performance of management (critical success factors)	Quarterly team meeting.
Financial performance	Cost centre and income performance produced monthly.
	Cash flow review and forecast produced quarterly.
	Audit and balance sheet produced at least annually.
	Income future forecast produced every six months.

● Managing changes involved in the plan

Mikhail Gorbachev looking back at the experience of perestroika talked about how key people did not change at all, instead they superficially adapted to it. They never fully accepted or committed themselves to the real changes involved in the project, they added some new words to their vocabulary, pretended to absorb it, but their practice and their behaviour remained the same.

INNOVATION IN NOT-FOR-PROFIT ORGANISATIONS

'…public service institutions find it far more difficult to innovate than even the most "bureaucratic" company. The "existing" seems to be even more of an obstacle.

'To be sure, every service institution likes to get bigger. In the absence of a profit test, size is the one criterion of success for a service institution and growth a goal in itself.

'And then, of course, there is always so much more that needs to be done. But stopping what has "always been done" and doing something new are equally anathema to service institutions, or at least excruciatingly painful to them.'

Peter Drucker 1984
reprinted with permission

An interesting way of looking at what changes are called for is the idea of first and second order change. First order change is change that takes place within the structure and culture as it currently exists. Second order changes require a profound change in how the organisation works if they are to take place at all. This is often called 'cultural change'.

EXAMPLES OF FIRST AND SECOND ORDER CHANGE

First order change	Second order change
Publishing a statement committing the organisation to 'user participation'.	Stopping doing something that has always been done, because users no longer want it.
Proclaiming that the organisation is committed to equal opportunities and putting on equality training sessions for staff.	Taking a risk with a new service to see if it is more relevant to a particular minority group.
Having a policy statement on good environmental practices.	Changing car mileage policies so as to encourage better use of environmental resources.
Writing a quality assurance manual that sets out minimum service standards.	Not taking on a low-fee contract, because you might not be able to keep to your quality standard.

Second order change often involves risk, considerable effort and sometimes anxiety and conflict. In looking at the implications of the business plan, the following points could be considered:

- What second order change is involved in the plan?
- What will be the risk involved in these changes?
- How can we best manage this change?
- How will we know that the change has been achieved?

There is a further exercise on first and second order change on p.89.

● Understanding strategic management

A survey of headteachers published in 1992 examined what they did with their time. A sample group of headteachers was asked to list what they considered to be the most important aspects of their role. Their list focused on 'strategic' issues, curriculum development, managing change, forward planning and school development. Detailed examination of what they actually did showed that the vast majority of their time at school was spent on fragmented tasks that no one else was available to do: repairing the photocopier, making a sign

or filling in for a sick colleague. It was as if all the strategic issues were continually pushed into taking a poor second or third place.

Different definitions of strategic management abound in management text books. The chart below sets out some of the differences between operational management (running the day-to-day work) and strategic management.

STRATEGIC AND OPERATIONAL MANAGEMENT

	Operational management	Strategic management
Focus	Day to day survival.	Long-term development of organisation.
Objective	Keeping things going.	Finding better ways of doing things or exploring new ideas.
Change	Coping with imposed change.	Managing change and transition.
Motive	Creating stability.	Creating future possibilities.
Purpose	Keeping current services functioning.	Exploring new services and ensuring future role.
Process	Use of procedures and systems.	Focus on evaluation, direction and vision.
Decision making	By precedent or rule book.	Considering future choices and options.

It is not about being either an operational manager or a strategic manager. Someone who was entirely operational in their management role would probably suffer from not seeing the 'big picture' and concentrate entirely on detail rather than the purpose. Equally, managers who focus entirely on strategic issues often lose touch with the realities of the organisation and are often dismissed as being aloof and impractical.

Strategic management in a voluntary organisation frequently involves the following six activities:

1 Making sure that everyone in and around the organisation understands the organisation's purpose and values.

2 Ensuring that the activities and projects connect together, that evaluation takes place, and that progress towards the mission and aims is measured.

3 Ensuring that the organisation keeps in touch with developments in the outside world. New needs, trends and opportunities are predicted and responded to.

4 Ensuring that the structures, systems and skills of the organisation fit the task and that the organisation is fit for its purpose.

5 Managing change that will affect the organisation. Increasingly the changes are not linear ones (i.e. getting from A to B), but are about managing uncertainty, where change is likely, but the details are not clear.

6 Coordinating and organising forward planning through identifying strategies, contingencies and business planning.

A problem frequently encountered as a result of a business planning exercise is what to do with activities that no longer fit the mission of the organisation and aims of the plan. Being ruthless is often not tolerated or particularly effective in the longer term. To keep running activities that are out of step with the rest of the organisation could eventually diminish the organisation's effort and leave it fragmented and drifting. Strategic management is often particularly difficult in such situations.

WHAT IF THINGS DO NOT FIT IN THE STRATEGY?

Many organisations have experienced difficulties in deciding what to do with activities and functions that are established parts of the organisation, but no longer fit with the direction agreed. The following are three examples of this:

1 A national children's charity was committed to non institutional care, but it still owned two large residential schools.
2 A voluntary organisation had a volunteer fundraising committee that raised annually decreasing amounts of money. The level of servicing and support it expected from the organisation made it hardly cost effective. The group was very reluctant to consider new ideas.
3 A charity decided to move into advocacy, campaigning and rights work. It still had a core of users who turned up most days expecting a social and recreational day centre.

Several strategies exist in this situation:

• Do nothing and hope that the activity will come to a natural end.
• Put the activity on a minimum 'care and contact' relationship in which time and money spent on it is tightly controlled.

• Plan an 'exit strategy', where over time the activity is phased out and resources redeployed.
• Merge it into another organisation or encourage it to 'float off' independently.
• Redirect it towards another purpose more in line with the current direction. If it is unable to make the change, after time, close it.

One manager observed that she spent more time dealing with the activities that did not fit the strategy than the ones that did. The following four points are useful in developing an 'exit strategy':

1 Keep the end date firmly in mind. Draw up a 'critical path' so that the end date is a central focus.
2 Keep people who work on, use and support the project well informed. Avoid surprises.
3 Organise a gradual programme of briefings, consultations, training, and support.
4 Look after the people involved. Acknowledge possible feelings of loss. Identify individual and group successes. Try to end it on a high point.

● Seven ways to use a business plan

Here are seven examples of how organisations can use a business plan and ensure that it does not become just another document that sits on the shelf.

1 As part of a management process
The business plan should be regularly used by managers to guide their actions and ensure that all activities contribute to the organisational strategy. At management team meetings and supervision sessions, managers should be using the business plan as a reference point.

2 To make potential funders and other backers feel confident
The business plan can play a key role in making potential funders feel confident that the organisation has the track record, experience and organisational foundations to properly deliver projects. The coordinator of a youth agency

described how she uses their business plan to 'show potential funders that we are an established, tried and tested organisation. I offer the plan to potential funders as a way of being proactive and showing that our house is in order'.

3 To help individuals and teams to plan
In a larger organisation the plan can be the starting point for individuals and teams to produce their own work plan. The business plan should set out the overall context and strategic direction. Individuals and teams should be able to demonstrate in their plans how their priorities and intentions should fit with the overall plan.

4 To monitor and share progress
The director of a community enterprise centre produces a quarterly update bulletin on progress achieved in implementing the plan. The bulletin is circulated to all staff, trustees and also to funding bodies. He commented that the

bulletin 'reminds people of what is in the plan, highlights its importance and, most of all, makes a positive statement that we are making progress and achieving things'.

5 To help people to understand the organisation

A good business plan should be able to help people understand the history, thinking and priorities behind the organisation. It can help new staff to see the bigger picture and how their work fits in.

6 To evaluate organisational success

The management board of an arts project revisits the business plan every management board meeting. A board member commented that 'the thirty minutes we spend on the plan is often the most useful – we look at progress, discuss blocks and agree adaptations to the plan. It is really important to identify and acknowledge progress in an organisation, especially when it is so easy to overlook it.

7 To develop partnerships and alliances

One agency uses its business plan as a way of creating alliances with other agencies doing similar work. The agency's manager sent out the plan to agencies doing similar work and invited comments on how joint working could be encouraged. Responses were such that a series of workshops were convened to encourage joint working and develop shared strategies. 'The business plan made clear our area of interest and expertise – other agencies could see how they fitted into it.'

TEN POINT CHECKLIST FOR MANAGEMENT COMMITTEES

How to keep the plan alive!

1   Regularly revisit the plan
Make sure that the plan is discussed at committee meetings. It can provide a useful tool to take stock on progress, ensure accountability and identify the need for new strategies.

2   Build strategy into all meetings
It's easy for a committee to spend all of its time on day-to-day reporting and operational matters. Try to ensure that meetings have a strategic dimension to them – reviewing current activities, future thinking and planning.

3   Make sure managers keep to the plan
The committee can help managers to deliver the plan by ensuring that they use the plan in their work. The plan should provide a guide for future development and action.

4   Develop some key performance indicators for the plan
The process of measurement will often help to ensure implementation. The regular collection, circulation and analysis of performance information will help to identify progress and also act as an early warning system of potential problems and blocks.

5   Set aside review sessions for the plan
At least once a year the committee should review the plan to check that the strategy is still relevant and being acted on.

6   Check that the assumptions behind the plan are still valid
In any planning process assumptions about the future are made (e.g. 'number of volunteers will remain the same'; 'referrals will stay at the same rate'). It is useful to record the main assumptions that you make, so that you can review them in the life of the plan. If the assumption proves to be incorrect the plan might need rethinking.

7   Focus on the plan's key priorities
Keep the plan's main priorities firmly on your agenda. Watch out for 'good ideas', urgent opportunities and other factors reducing your focus. The hard part of having priorities is saying what you are not going to do.

8   Highlight success
When elements of the plan have been successfully completed make a point of letting people know. The process of recording progress and sharing success can increase morale internally and also increase the confidence of external stakeholders such as funders.

9   Circulate the plan to new committee members
As new people join the committee, ensure that they are given the plan and have an opportunity to talk it through. The plan can be a valuable way of learning about the organisation and understanding the work in hand.

10   Don't allow drift
It is easy for an organisation to drift from issue to issue or be driven by other people's priorities. Make sure that everyone in the organisation understands the strategy and manage carefully the temptation to add things in. If you need to change the strategy, do so formally, make clear what is coming out as well as what is going in.

▼ Exercise 19

EXAMPLE OF AN IMPLEMENTATION PLANNER

The implementation planner is used to ensure that resources, timescales and a review process are clearly agreed and recorded for each part of the strategy. The planner should be drawn up by the person responsible for leading the priority and be formally approved. It is worthwhile to bring all the individual planners together to ensure that there is coordination in the organisation and to avoid clashes over resources.

Strategic priority

To investigate the feasibility of developing community businesses in the area

---

Person responsible

Development officer

reporting to

Director

Key outcomes:

1 To establish whether a community business model would assist in the economic regeneration of the area.
2 To support and develop existing community businesses in the area and ensure their long-term viability and growth.
3 To develop a support network for local community businesses.

Workplan

Task	start date	review date	end date
1 To carry out an initial audit	Jan 01	March 01	April 01
2 To run an awareness day	– scheduled for Feb 01		
3 To explore funding support	Jan 01	March 01	April 01 June 01
4 To set up resource library	Feb 01	April 01	
5 To do needs assessment on existing businesses	Feb 01	April 01	June 01
6 To set up support network	March 01	June 01	Sept 01
7 To produce strategy plan	April 01		July 01

Resources allocated

Development officer's time – 30 days of work plan

Support from Director, Admin officer, Information officer

£500 from development budget for travel, materials, etc.

Review date

Progress report to management committee in March and June

Committee to make decision on future feasibility in July

IMPLEMENTATION PLANNER

Strategic priority

Person responsible   **reporting to**

Key outcomes:

Workplan
Task   **start date**   **review date**   **end date**

Resources allocated

Review date

▼ Exercise 20

'SOFT' STRATEGY MISSING?

A theatre had invested substantial time and money in producing a business plan. External consultants, residential weekends and considerable extra work by the finance officer had produced a final document. The plan looked impressive, with detailed objectives, cash flow projections and measurable business targets.

Three months after the plan's production the theatre's director announced her intention to resign and live abroad. The announcement did not surprise anyone, as for the past year she had often talked about her plans. The director had set the theatre up and in many respects it was an extension of her personality. Much of the theatre's 'know how' was carried in her head. She had a considerable personal network of funders, contacts and supporters. Trustees and staff expressed fear and panic about the difficulty of replacing her and how much would be lost when she left.

The organisation had spent nearly a whole year planning. All the hard elements (costing, marketing plans, staffing levels) had been properly dealt with, but one of the few things that could have been anticipated had been ignored. This is an example of soft strategy.

Soft strategy could include elements such as: people, styles of work, goodwill, cooperation and partnerships.

What elements of soft strategy need to be thought about in your planning process?

▼ Exercise 21

SCENARIO PLANNING

Several organisations, notably in the military and the oil industry, have used imaginary scenarios as both a learning and planning tool. A possible future situation is described and participants work out how the organisation could respond to it, and then evaluate the likely impact of their actions.

A housing organisation developed its annual staff residential weekend around three scenarios:

1. The decision by a major funder to withdraw its financial commitment by phasing it out over two years.
2. A change in the political control and the managerial style within a local authority. The new leadership would be interested in partnerships and transferring the management of several projects from the public to the independent sectors.
3. A decline in demand. A combination of reasons have led to a sharp fall in the numbers of referrals to a usually busy project. Financial, marketing and service plans would need to be quickly implemented.

Staff worked in teams to suggest short-term and long-term action plans, explore options, spot dangers and test out the organisation's current processes.

Extensive discussion followed on how the scenarios could have been anticipated or avoided, the importance of a coordinated response throughout the organisation and the need for contingency plans.

The outcome of the day was that all staff had some experience of strategic thinking, and several outline contingency plans were produced (for example, blueprints for possible projects should the opportunity arise).

Three months after the exercise, a similar situation to one of the scenarios did arise which tested the effectiveness of the plans and the process!

What scenarios could you design for your organisation?

What would be your organisation's likely response?

Chaotic?	**Coordinated?**	**Delayed?**
Strategic?	**Planned?**	**Bureaucratic?**

▼ Exercise 22

MONITORING THE PLAN

This exercise will help you to monitor the progress of the plan
and evaluate its longer-term effectiveness.

What are the key milestones that can be used to monitor the plan's progress?

How and when will the following elements of the plan be reviewed and monitored?

	How will it be monitored and reviewed?	Frequency
Mission		
Are the assumptions in the plan still valid?		
Are the strategic aims still the right ones?		
Progress/outcome of each aim.		
Progress report on each objective.		
Performance of management (delivery of the critical success factors).		
Financial performance.		
Performance to plan of each project/ cost centre.		
Overall financial performance		

In terms of outcomes and results how will you judge the plan's overall success?

▼ Exercise 23

MAKING THE PLAN WORK

This exercise aims to help you to identify the factors that the people responsible for managing the plan will have to develop. As you work through the exercises, note down any factor, process or attribute that you feel will be needed to successfully implement the plan.

1   All organisations have high points and low points. Draw a line of the organisation's history (or at least for as long as you have known it).

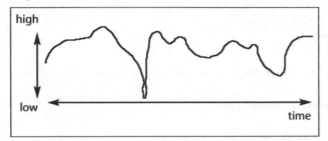

What criteria did you use to judge if something was a 'high' or a 'low' point?

List the factors that created the organisational high points or helped it recover from a low point.

2   Think of successful organisations that you know well. What are the factors that contribute to their success? Focus on internal factors and external factors.

Are any of these factors available to you in implementing your plan?

3   Organisations are usually described in structural terms (departments, units etc.). Often the key to success is getting the key processes right. Processes usually cut across an organisation's structure and depend upon cooperation, team work and communication.

In terms of your plan what processes does the organisation need to get right?

Review your list. Try to identify a limited number (no more than eight) critical success factors that your organisation needs to focus on to successfully implement the plan.

▼ **Exercise 24**

THE IMPLICATIONS OF THE PLAN

Divide likely changes involved as a result of the plan into 'first order' and 'second order' changes. First order changes are changes that can be absorbed or managed within the current organisation's structures and culture. Second order changes are those that are likely to require change in the way that you work. List the kind of changes that might be involved, under the seven headings used by the McKinsey's 7-S framework (see p.31).

	first order change	second order change
Strategy (direction and priorities)		
Structure (organisational design)		
Staff (employment practices)		
Skills (competence and skill gaps)		
Systems (financial and management controls)		
Style (relations to users and image)		
Shared values (what is important about how we work)		

FURTHER READING

Titles published by the Directory of Social Change (DSC) and Charities Aid Foundation (CAF) are available from the Directory of Social Change, Publications department, 24 Stephenson Way, London NW1 2DP.
Call 08450 77 77 07 or e-mail: publications@dsc.org.uk for more details and for a free publications list, which can also be viewed at the DSC website: www.dsc.org.uk

DSC also runs courses on organisational development and management. For details, contact the Training department on 020 7209 4949, or e-mail training@dsc.org.uk

● Strategic management issues

The Strategic Management Blueprint
Paul Dobson & Ken Starkey
Blackwell Business Books
1st edition 1993
ISBN 0 631186 24 7

Strategic Management
Cliff Bowman & David Asch
Palgrave (*formerly Macmillan Press*)
1st edition 1987
ISBN 0 333387 65 1

Innovation and Entrepreneurship
Peter F Drucker
Pan
ISBN 0 330 29465 2
(*New edition 1999*
Butterworth-Heinemann
ISBN 0 750643 88 9)

Learning to Lead
Bob Garratt
Harper Collins
1st edition 1990
ISBN 0 00 637722 X

Developing your Organisation
Alan Lawrie
DSC
1st edition 2000
ISBN 1 900360 66 7

● Business planning

Planning for the Future
Nicholas Martin & Caroline Smith
NCVO
1st edition 1993
ISBN 0 719913 74 8

The Business Plan Workbook
Robert Brown, Colin Barrow & Paul Barrow
Kogan Page
4th edition 2001
ISBN 0 749434 99 6

● Financial issues

A Practical Guide to Accounting by Charities
Kate Sayer
DSC
1st edition 1996
ISBN 1 873860 95 1

A Practical Guide to Financial Management for Charities
Kate Sayer
DSC
1st edition 1998
ISBN 1 873860 84 6

● Related issues

Managing the Non-profit Organisation
Peter F Drucker
Butterworth-Heinemann
1995 (UK edition)
ISBN 0 750626 91 7

Outcome Funding
Harold S Williams & Arthur Y Webb
NCVO
1992 (UK edition)
ISBN 0 7199 1378 0

INDEX